THE OTIS REDDING STORY

Other Signal Books You Will Enjoy

THE OTIS REDDING STORY

by Jane Schiesel

f. 58736

1973
DOUBLEDAY & COMPANY, INC., GARDEN CITY, NEW YORK

Grateful acknowledgment is made to Atlantic Records
for the use of the jacket photo
and to Stax-Volt Records
for the use of the frontispiece photo

ISBN: 0-385-02335-9
Library of Congress Catalog Card Number 70–144294
Copyright © 1973 by Doubleday & Company, Inc.
All Rights Reserved
Printed in the United States of America

Prepared by 🅱 Rutledge Books
First Edition

CONTENTS

Chapter 1

GONNA MAKE IT

Sundays. Black, soulful Sundays. Nine-year-old Otis Redding, Jr., was shouting out hymns with the rest of the Mount Ivy Baptist Church in Macon, Georgia, while the pastor, Otis Redding, Sr., led the small congregation in song.

When Reverend Redding said, "Now, brothers and sisters, let us pray," the church members bowed their heads. Otis, Jr., his dark brown forehead wrinkled with concentration, prayed this Sunday for the same thing he prayed for every Sunday: money.

Otis Redding had already decided that he didn't like being poor. He didn't like to see his five brothers and sisters going around in worn-out hand-me-down clothes. He didn't like to see his mother stuffing rags in the cracks of their four-room shanty to try to keep out the cold in winter. And he hated to see his father, who was a farmer when he wasn't a preacher, struggling to grow

7

something in the poor soil only to produce barely enough to pay his share to the white landowner.

So Otis prayed for money. But young as he was, he'd also already learned the proverb that the Lord helps those who help themselves. He didn't intend to just sit around and wait for divine intervention to bring him wealth. He liked to sing, and he liked everything that had to do with music. He knew all the songs in the hymnal, including the harmonizing lines, and he had a knack for learning and arranging songs. A year before, when he was only eight, he had organized a children's choir that was so good they had been invited to sing in other nearby towns. And Otis had a plan. Right from the beginning, Otis never simply hoped or prayed for anything. He always had a plan.

By 1954, when he was thirteen, Otis' interest in gospel music had evolved into an interest in rhythm and blues and in rock and roll. One afternoon after school he was listening to a disc by Little Richard:

> Gonna tell Aunt Mary 'bout Uncle John,
> He says he has the miseries but he's havin'
> a lot of fun.

Otis fiddled with the knobs on the beat-up phonograph, but it was no use. The sound coming out was the best that could be expected from a machine that had been used as long as this one had.

When the forty-five ended, Otis flipped it over and played the other side. This time when Little Richard started to sing, Otis sang along with him. Fingers snapping, his body moving and turning in time to the music, Otis sang all the words, made all the sounds he heard on the record. He could stay with the rocking up-beat tempo, shoot out the lyrics like bullets from a machine gun, and scream and shout just like Little Richard did.

Otis liked a lot of singers, but he felt really close to Little Richard because Richard was from his hometown, Macon, and Macon was a swinging place when it came to soul music. Someone was always sponsoring a talent show, and most of the local nightclubs used Macon talent. Little Richard had started there, and if Richard had made it, Otis was sure he could, too.

The stack of forty-fives slid over when the vibrations from Otis' movements got to be too much for the rickety table, and he stopped to pick them up. Little Richard. Dee Clark. James Brown and the Flames. The Charms. Sam Cooke. These were Otis' favorite artists, and he had nearly all of their records.

Every day when he got home from his after-school job Otis settled down with these sides. He listened to the tunes over and over, learning the words, making up movements, analyzing the rhythms. Since he didn't have any money for formal music lessons, he used his records to teach himself. Every chance he got he'd practice on the piano in the school auditorium, trying to re-create the chords and melodies he heard on the forty-fives. He was also trying to teach himself to play the guitar and drums, when he had the chance, which wasn't often.

The record came to a scratchy end, and as Otis lifted the arm to play the tune again he heard his mother call him.

"Otis, turn off that record player, for goodness' sake, and come do an errand for me."

"Okay, okay," Otis mumbled as he carefully placed the records and the phonograph on a shelf.

Mrs. Redding pointed to a large box on the table. "Take this down to Mrs. Sims, Otis. And I wish you'd stop playing those records so much. You know how your father feels about them."

Otis sighed but didn't say anything. He just picked up the box and swung out into the night air.

It was a beautiful night—the sky was clear and the stars were shining through the tall Georgia pines. The smell of those pines filled Otis with a good feeling. He loved the South. Everybody he cared about—his family, his friends—was here. The farmland that his father worked on so hard was here. And all that good soul music was here.

Passing horses grazing in a field, Otis promised himself that one day he'd buy a ranch right near Macon where his father could farm, with good livestock and equipment, and where Otis could keep a whole corral of horses. And he knew that the ranch and the music were both part of the same dream.

He shifted the box under his arm. Up ahead he saw the Sims house, and he noticed Claude Sims's car parked out in front. Claude, the Sims's oldest son, owned one of the weekend night spots in town.

Otis hadn't seen Claude for a while, but he'd been thinking about talking to him. The next thing in Otis' plan was to try to break into nightclub work, and he wanted to ask Claude about appearing at his place. "No time like the present," Otis said to himself.

Mrs. Sims greeted Otis at the door and thanked him for the package.

"How you doing?" Claude asked as he moved over on the couch to make room for Otis. "Heard you sing at the dance at the school last Wednesday. You're doing all right."

"I try," Otis replied. "You know, just keep on pushin'."

"When you gonna be singing again?" Claude asked.

"Well, you know, I sing every day." Otis smiled. "But if you mean, when am I gonna perform again, I don't know. I don't have anything definite. You know, Claude, I sure would dig a chance to sing at your club—you know, to work for a real audience, not just kids or talent shows."

Claude frowned a little. "I don't know, Otis. You're kinda young."

"That don't mean anything," Otis said firmly. "I'm a good singer, everybody likes me. I'm willing to work, and I can put on a good act. That's what's important, not how old I am."

"You got me there," Claude said. "It's funny, just the other day somebody asked me whether I'd ever thought of hiring you for a Friday night . . ."

"Well then, how about it?"

"Can you have an act together by Friday?"

"My act is always together," Otis said.

"Okay. The band practices every evening at the club. There are some instruments—a guitar, a set of drums— in the back, and a piano out front, and if you want to practice alone you can. Just drop by the record shop next door and pick up the key. You can see Hank, the leader of the group, about rehearsing your set with them."

Otis was delighted. He'd been borrowing a friend's

guitar to practice on from time to time. The chords he was picking out sounded pretty good, but he just hadn't had enough time with the instrument. Now he'd have a chance to practice with a guitar all week. Not only that, he could tighten up his hand on the drums and piano, too.

Otis asked Claude how much he was willing to pay.

"I've only got a little place, Otis, so I can't offer you much. Let's say fifteen dollars for this first go 'round and then we'll see what happens from there."

Only fifteen dollars—that was no way to start saving to buy a guitar, much less his own ranch, Otis thought. It looked like show business was going to be a scuffle. But he knew if he was going to make it he'd better take everything that came along, especially if there was nothing better. And right now there was nothing better.

"Okay, man, it's a deal. I'll start working with the group tomorrow night."

As Otis got up to leave, Mrs. Sims, who had been sitting quietly sewing, spoke up. "Don't know how your father's going to take this, Otis," she said, slowly shaking her head. "He doesn't much abide by people going to nightclubs. I don't think he'll like his son singing in one."

"I've got to do the thing I can do best, Mrs. Sims," Otis replied softly, "and that's singing. And if I'm gonna make it as a singer I've got to sing where there's money. There's some money in clubs and there's more money on the stage, and so that's where I've got to go."

"Well, I still say it's something you better think about," Mrs. Sims said.

Otis cut school all that week so he could get his thing together to be ready to rehearse with the club band every night, and somehow he avoided talking with his father about this new development. By Friday night, Otis was calm. He and the band at the club had the act together, and he was going to come on like a professional.

After Otis' second set Claude's club was humming with good feeling, and Claude knew his customers were really digging Otis "Rocking" Redding. At the end of the evening the feeling was even better, and Claude spoke to Otis about working there on a regular basis.

"There were people here from some of the other clubs in town, and a couple of them were talking about getting you for their places," Claude said, "so I guess I better get my bid in early."

That really pleased Otis. "Well, do you think I'm worth a raise, then?" he asked, smiling.

Claude broke out laughing. "Otis, you're really something. Okay, how about twenty-five a night?"

Otis paused for a second. "Okay, man," he said coolly. "That sounds good for the time being."

It was after one in the morning before Otis left the club, and although he got a ride with one of the guys in the band it was past one-thirty when they pulled up in front of his house. Otis was surprised to see lights still on—usually everyone was asleep by this time.

He tore up the steps, and when he opened the front door he saw his father sitting in the front room. Reverend Redding was holding the Bible. His face looked tired, but his eyes were bright and determined. He was very angry.

"Otis, sit down over here. I want to talk to you."

Otis' father had never liked his son's rhythm and blues records, and when Otis had started singing in talent shows his father hadn't been happy about that either. Now Otis was singing in a nightclub, and that was really going too far, his father thought.

According to Reverend Redding, nightclubs were outside the limits of God's realm. They were places of sin, and if Otis helped keep them going by singing in them, Reverend Redding said, then Otis was sinning too.

"But, Pop," Otis explained, "I've got to start getting some club jobs if I'm ever gonna make it in show business, if I'm gonna have a career."

"Career?" his father shot back. "You talkin' about screamin' around the house with those records and runnin' off to some talent shows? That ain't no career. It ain't nothin' but teen-age foolishness."

"Look, I'm serious about singing," Otis answered quietly. "I've won in those talent shows, and I can sing as good as those people on the records. I know I can make a lot of money and do what I most want to do."

"No need making money if you're going to lose your soul because of it. You even been cutting school, I hear, for this nonsense. Next thing I know you won't be going to school at all, or church either!"

"Pop, singing is as important to me as preaching is to you. I got to sing the way you got to preach."

Reverend Redding looked even more tired. "Well, I don't think you're as grown-up as you seem to think, but I know it ain't no use trying to stop you," he said. "I'm going to tell you something, Otis. You won't ever amount to anything with this singing, this hanging out in nightclubs, not a thing. And I'm going to tell you something else. Whether you make it or not, I'm never going to go see you in one of those places."

Otis looked directly at his father. "Pop, I know you can't understand it, but I've got to do it. I'm gonna make it, and I'm gonna stay straight, and someday you'll be proud of me."

Chapter 2

OL' RELIABLE

"Man, look at that fool go on the guitar," Otis said to the other tèen-age performers who were waiting back-stage at the Douglas Theater in Macon one night in 1956.

"He can play, all right," someone answered.

"Who's the group?"

"Pat Teacake and the Panthers. The guy playin' that funky guitar is Johnny Jenkins."

Otis really dug the sounds. The guitarist was together —he had technique, but he also had soul, and he didn't miss a thing. The drummer was okay, too. He had a good, strong, steady beat, the kind Otis liked to feel under him when he sang.

The group finished the number with Johnny Jenkins doing some far-out chords, and the audience stomped its approval as the MC danced out onto the stage.

"Can you dig *that?*" he yelled.

"Yeah!" the crowd shouted back.

"I can't hear you," the MC yelled. "I said, can you *dig* it?"

And again a roar of "YEAH!" rolled up from the audience.

"That's more like it—now we can go on with this marathon. 'Cause you know we're gonna jam here all day and half the night if they'll let us!"

Jamming all day—that's what a marathon was all about. Bands playing and people singing until the audience finally decided who was the best singer and which was the best band. But for Otis this wasn't only another chance to win first-prize money, but to perform for his largest audience so far—the show was being broadcast over a local radio station.

Pat Teacake and his group brushed past Otis as they left the stage.

"Hey, man, you really sounded okay out there," Otis said.

"Thanks," Cake replied.

"You didn't sound so bad yourself," Johnny Jenkins said to Otis.

"Yeah, my first set was all right, I guess, but the house band here isn't saying anything. They're a little shaky on the tempo. I want the beat fast, but I want those accented beats to come down like a sledge-hammer." He pounded his fist into his open palm.

"Like Little Richard's group does it," added Johnny.

"You got it. I was wondering while you were out there if you all could back me up on my next set. It'd sure be better than working with the theater band."

"You know, that's a terrific idea. Hey, Cake," Johnny called. "Come here a minute. How about backing Otis on his next set?"

"No, man, can't do it," Cake replied, almost before Johnny had even asked the question.

Otis felt his muscles tighten.

"Why not?" Johnny asked.

"Well, you know, a lot of reasons," Cake mumbled, looking at the floor.

"Such as?" Johnny persisted.

"Well, the cat's kinda inexperienced, isn't he? We don't want to tie our act to an amateur."

"He's no amateur, man!" Johnny answered. "He's the best singer in Macon. I've seen his act at some of the clubs and so have you, Cake. You know Otis puts every-thing he's got into a number."

"Well, he's too young," Cake continued. "I bet he's hardly fifteen."

"I don't care if he's fifteen or fifty—it doesn't make any difference. He can deliver a song. Look, the audience was practically standing on their seats when he finished his first set. It might even help *our* image to work with him."

Otis realized the band's leader had the right to decide whom he wanted to perform with, and he knew it was better if he didn't butt in. But he was getting angry and had to restrain himself.

"Besides," Johnny went on, "he sure doesn't look anybody's fifteen."

That was certainly true. Otis was over six feet tall, with a broad, husky build and a voice that was strong enough to be heard all the way from Macon to Atlanta. And as soon as he came on stage, the girls in the audience would start clapping and calling out his name. Maybe, Otis thought, *that* was what was bothering Cake —he didn't want that kind of competition.

"Come on, how about it?" Johnny asked.

"Well, I don't know . . ." Cake mumbled.

"Look, it's like this," Johnny said firmly. "*I* want to play with Otis. Do the rest of you fellows want to?" he asked the other members of the group, who were standing around.

A chorus of "Yeah" and "He sings all right" and "Let's do it" was the reply.

"All right, that's the way it is, Cake," Johnny concluded. "Sorry, but you're out-voted. We'll work with Otis on his next set and see how it goes."

"Groovy, man," Otis said softly, smiling.

By the time Otis was to go on again, the group was ready. They had practiced backstage during intermission, and Otis and Johnny fit together hand in glove.

When the MC announced that Otis "Rocking" Redding and Pat Teacake and the Panthers were going to be teaming up, the theater filled with applause. And when Otis bounded out onto the stage and started singing, some of the girls screamed and a few couples began dancing in the aisles. Then when Johnny joined in it was too much. They finished their number and the crowd called for more, so they launched right into a second. The crowd liked that even better and yelled for another. Otis was really rocking now, dancing up and down the stage and belting out the lyrics. When they finally wrapped up their last tune, the MC knew he didn't even have to ask who'd get the prize money.

"That was *some* set," Johnny said backstage as he and Otis splashed water on their hot faces.

"You know it." Otis smiled back. "By the way, Johnny, I didn't get a real chance to thank you for sticking up for me with Cake."

"Oh, think nothin' of it."

"But I *am* thinking about it. I'm gonna make it to the

top, man, and I'm not gonna forget my friends when I get there."

Johnny looked at Otis for a long minute and then he broke into a grin! "Give me five on that, partner." The two slapped flat palms together.

Otis sang with the Panthers for several months, but Cake became more and more hostile toward him, and it was hard to get a good groove going. Finally, Otis and Johnny decided to form their own group. They got several other local musicians together and called themselves Johnny Jenkins and the Pinetoppers. Otis was the lead singer with the group.

It was a good move for Otis. He'd been working quite a bit since his first professional gig at Claude Sims's club, but he'd had to work with whatever group was appearing at a club or with house bands in theaters. This was his first chance to play with a group steadily and work out some things he really wanted to do.

He'd dropped out of school—after a lot of hassles with his parents, especially his father—but he'd had a chance to get the guitar and drums and piano together, as well as his singing, and he was starting to write more and more of the songs he sang. His melodies were simple and the lyrics uncomplicated, which was the way he liked it. Later, in an interview, he put it like this:

"Basically I like any music that remains simple and

22

I feel this is the formula that has made soul music successful. When any music form becomes cluttered or complicated you lose the average listener's ear. There's nothing more beautiful than a simple blues tune. There's beauty in simplicity whether you're talking about architecture, art, or music."

Otis' tunes weren't too different from the gospel music he'd sung in his father's church, but they were charged with the pounding beat that was the trademark of rhythm and blues. His sound was popular with his audiences, but it wasn't very original. He still sounded a lot like Little Richard, especially on the up-tempo numbers, but he was also getting more and more into the kind of less frantic thing Sam Cooke did. He was starting to do some slow, ultra-soulful ballads, and gradually he was developing his own sound. But he still had a way to go, and he knew it.

The group always rehearsed at Johnny's house. For one thing, the Jenkins home was less crowded than Otis', and for another, Johnny had a cute next-door neighbor named Zelma, who often dropped by when they were practicing.

Zelma was a small girl with chestnut eyes that always seemed to light up her oval face. Otis wanted to tell her that he liked the way she looked when she was listening to him sing, but for some reason he was even quieter than usual when she was around.

"Hey, Johnny, how about this?" Otis asked one afternoon when he and Johnny were rehearsing. "I made it up on the way home last night."

Otis picked out the melody on his guitar and sang the lyrics:

> Now that you left me, good lord how I cry,
> You don't miss the water till the well runs dry.

"Give it to me again," Johnny said, moving in closer.

Otis went through the number once more, and Johnny started to pick it up. When they finished, Otis smiled.

"Sure didn't waste any time getting into that."

"You write 'em and I'll play 'em," Johnny responded.

"That's where it's at," Otis replied.

"Do you think we'll have it together for our club date in Chester this weekend?" Johnny asked.

"If we keep on like this, we will."

Just then Zelma walked in. "Hi, Johnny, Otis. How you doing?"

"Zelma, you got to hear this new number Otis wrote," Johnny said enthusiastically, not even saying hello.

Otis plunked a few chords on his guitar. Right now

he couldn't think of a thing to say except, "C'mon, Johnny. Let's get this tune together."

Johnny played the opening chords. Otis stood in the middle of the living room floor, and when he started to sing he was very aware that Zelma was watching and listening. It seemed that all his shyness melted away when he opened his mouth to sing. He clapped his hands, moving around the room, and when he reached the words "Now that you've left me," he swung around in a full circle and pointed to Zelma.

Suddenly Johnny stopped playing. "Otis, I just don't seem to be able to get that part right."

"Here, man, let me show you," Otis said, taking the guitar. Perching on the arm of a chair, he became that one-man band that never failed to amaze people when they saw it: Otis playing the guitar line, humming the melody, and beating out the rhythm with his feet. Nearly every song he performed started out with him putting it together like that.

"Yeah, I hear what you mean. I'll keep workin' at it," Johnny said when Otis finished. "It'll be together by Friday night."

"But will that car of yours be together by Friday night?" Zelma asked, with a grin.

"You would have to mention that," said Johnny, slouching down in his chair.

The battered Buick the Pinetoppers used on their gigs was a disaster. It looked bad, sounded bad, and sometimes, when the exhaust pipe shook loose, smelled bad. The car barely made it to local clubs—how was it going to make it all the way to Chester?

"Zelma's right," Otis said. "We better put in a lot of time on that car this week or we'll be doing our act in the middle of noplace."

So all that week the Pinetoppers worked on both the car and their numbers.

"Otis, I think she needs a new generator," said the drummer, Sammy, after he'd been exploring the engine.

Otis looked out from under the car. "I guess we've got to get one, then," he said.

"But where we gonna get the bread?" Johnny asked, frowning.

Money was a problem. When the group had been organized, all the musicians had pooled their funds so they could get some uniforms, some equipment, and this beat-up car. Now they were all broke, because they didn't make much on their gigs. Otis was frowning, too.

"Well, since I'm working part time at a junkyard," he said, "maybe I can dig up a good second-hand generator there."

"Yeah, man. Otherwise we can forget Chester."

"We *have* to make it to Chester," Otis declared. "I'm not missing any gigs."

Since Otis had left school, he'd had various jobs—cleaning yards, repairing wells, painting fences—and now he was working in a junkyard to try to make the money he couldn't make strictly as an entertainer. And although he didn't like to ask for favors from his employers, he couldn't pass up this opportunity. So when he went into work the next day he explained the problem to the owner of the yard, a sympathetic man who knew about the group Otis worked with.

"Sure, Otis, I've probably got some generators in the shed," he said. "Why don't you take a look?"

"Hey, thanks. I'll look around. I really appreciate it."

Otis finally found a generator that would fit the Buick, and since it looked better than the one they had, he took it. The Pinetoppers put the generator in their car and did as much else as they could to get it into shape. By Friday afternoon it was as ready as it would ever be.

"Hey, see what time it is," Otis said to Johnny after they'd finished with the car.

"A little after four," Johnny replied.

"We'd better get on the road, then," said Otis, "so we can be there in plenty of time to see what the layout is and practice a while."

After they cleaned up, the Pinetoppers went through

their usual routine of loading the car—putting drums, amplifiers, instruments, and all the other paraphernalia they had to carry with them in the trunk and on a beat-up luggage rack on top of the car. And then somehow all seven of them jammed inside with whatever stuff they couldn't fit anyplace else. It was quite a sight.

"We should make it in about two hours," Johnny said as he adjusted the rearview mirror so he could see over all the heads in the back seat. Johnny did the driving, and Otis sat next to him, always with a pencil and paper.

If he heard anything he particularly dug on the R&B station on the radio, he'd write it down—not the actual notes, since he didn't know how to write music, but the name of the tune, which would be enough to remind him of what it was that had attracted him about the piece. But he didn't just get ideas from other songs—he often heard things he liked in commercials. The "bloop bloop bloop bloop" of the Maxwell House coffee commercial, for example, found its way into a number of Otis' horn arrangements, and when "Sweet Soul Music" hit the charts few people make the connection between its theme and the Marlboro cigarette commercial.

"Don't push it, Johnny," Otis said with a smile.

"Push it? Man, if I try to make this thing go over

forty she'll sit right down in the middle of the road and quit."

"Are we really only getting three hundred bucks for this gig?" Sammy asked from the back seat.

"That's right—that's all I could get out of the club owner," Otis replied. "We really need a manager to do our negotiating."

Otis had been thinking about the problem of getting a manager for quite a while. Three hundred dollars came out to $42.85 for each man for playing for six hours, rehearsing ten, fifteen, sometimes twenty hours a week, and keeping their instruments and outfits in good repair. It was really chicken feed.

Things might really begin to shape up if we had a manager, Otis thought, but it would have to be a good one. He'd heard too many stories of managers who picked up the group's pay and left town. So he felt it was best to wait until they found the right person, someone who'd really work for the group. Then he'd be free to spend more time writing music and perfecting the act instead of being so involved in the business end of things.

Otis was shaken out of his thoughts when Johnny violently tugged at the wheel of the car and steered it to the side of the road. The engine sputtered and went dead.

"We've had it!" Johnny said.

"Think we ran out of gas?" That was Jimmy, the pianist and "comedian" in the group.

"Very funny. I wish that's all there was to it," Otis said. Everybody got out and stood around looking at the car.

Johnny groaned. "We're closer to Macon than we are to Chester. Maybe we better forget it."

"No, man," Otis said. "Those people are paying for a show, they're expecting a show, and they're going to get a show."

"But how we gonna get there? It'll take us until tomorrow to walk," Jimmy protested.

"Give me some tools," Otis said as he lifted the hood of the car. "Doesn't look like anything wrong here," he said, taking off his jacket.

"What are you doing, man?" Johnny asked.

"I'm gonna check out underneath," Otis answered, and slid under the car.

"Otis, you're gonna get filthy!"

Finally Otis dragged himself out and stood up, looking thoughtful.

"Didn't find anything?" Jimmy asked.

"Nope, not yet." Otis walked around to look under the hood again. Suddenly he shouted. "How could I have been so dumb? We didn't bolt the generator tight enough. It's shaken loose."

He worked on it and then asked Johnny to try the engine again. Johnny got in and turned on the ignition. The motor started with a roar, then settled into its normal sputtering. The group joked as they climbed back into the car.

"Outta sight, Otis," said Johnny as Otis slid into the front seat.

"Talk about outta sight," said Jimmy. "Take a look at the big man's pants!" They were smeared with dirt and oil stains.

"Oh well," Otis said, turning to smile at Jimmy. "Never mind. I told you we weren't going to miss a gig, and we're not going to."

Chapter 3

BLUE-EYED SOUL

It was 1957, midsummer.

Otis grabbed the mike and danced back and forth across the small outdoor stage.

"Don't leave me, baby," he wailed to the audience of teenagers in Macon's Lakeside Park.

The park was a summer hangout for the white kids of the area, and every weekend the manager of Lakeside hired local bands to perform. Tonight Johnny Jenkins and the Pinetoppers, with Otis Redding, were playing. Most of the kids had never heard of the group, or of Otis.

Otis delivered his numbers as though there were no tomorrow. Johnny was going wild on the guitar, and the whole group was really with it. When they finished their last number the park erupted with sounds of clapping and hooting and calls for more. The group launched into an encore, everybody around the bandstand swaying and clapping and dancing again. Everybody, that is, except Phil Walden, a blue-eyed, red-haired eighteen-year-old who had been standing motionless by the bandstand ever since the Pinetoppers had begun their set.

The group finished their encore and again the crowd roared for more. That Otis fever had gotten to them, that fever that infected all Redding audiences. Every person out there knew he was singing just to them, just for them. And with every word, shout and holler, Otis charged them up higher and higher until you could feel the sparks in the air.

"Say, who's the singer with your group?" Phil asked Johnny as he jumped down from the stage.

"That's ol' Rockin' Otis Redding," Johnny replied.

"He sure can sing, can't he?"

"You ain't kiddin'," Johnny said, shaking his head and wiping his glistening face with a handkerchief.

"You know," Johnny continued, "if they let him, the guy'd sing all day *and* all night! He's a powerhouse."

Just then Otis walked up. "Man, we really turned them on, didn't we?" he said to Johnny.

"Yeah. At this rate, we'll just play our way to glory," Johnny laughed.

"I was just telling Johnny what a great singer you are," Phil said.

"Thanks," Otis replied, noticing Phil for the first time. "That's all I like to do and that's all I want to do."

"Do you fellows have a manager?" Phil asked.

"No, not really," Otis said. "Why—you know somebody?"

"Well, you see, I book some rhythm and blues acts in the area, and I'd like to book you, if you're willing," Phil answered.

This was the last thing Otis had expected—a white boy asking to be his manager. They introduced themselves and then Otis asked, "Man, how'd you get into soul music?"

"When my brother came home from the Army he brought some soul records with him. I really dug the sounds. You know, James Brown, Ray Charles, LaVerne Baker, the Clovers, groups like that."

"They can wail," Otis agreed.

"You know it. Well, at first I thought I'd get into rhythm and blues singing myself."

Otis' eyebrows went up. A white boy singing soul?

"Man, I practiced and practiced," Phil went on, "but no matter how hard I tried, I couldn't even stay on pitch, much less sound anything like James Brown."

Otis couldn't help but let out a chuckle.

"It was funny, all right," Phil said, grinning too. "It was impossible, but I wanted to be in the soul-music business so bad that I decided to do the next best thing—manage R&B groups. Right now I've got several black groups. Mostly I try to arrange bookings at white colleges and at clubs where they can get a little better bread."

Otis asked Phil who the groups were that he booked and Phil told him. Then they got into a heavy discussion about the R&B scene in general—what made one group different from another, why one singer seemed to be making it while somebody very similar wasn't, what it was about the music that seemed to get to the audiences, the differences between "live" and recorded performances.

"Hey, Otis, time for us to get back onstage," Johnny called.

"Right away, man," Otis called back.

We need the exposure and better money, and this guy might be able to open up some new doors, Otis thought—and he sure seems to know his stuff.

Before he went back on the stand, Otis said, "Okay, Phil. You find the gigs. We'll work any place, any time." They shook hands on the agreement.

Otis, Phil, and Johnny all worked on finding bookings. Sometimes there would be a spot just for Otis, sometimes for the whole group, but Otis sang every chance he got. He worked the "soul circuit" in the area, singing at all the talent shows and amateur nights. Sometimes he packed the audience with his friends so they'd vote for him and then he split the take with them afterward. He also sang at the nearby white colleges and high schools and at places like disabled veterans' clubs. He'd meant it when he said he'd work anywhere any time he could.

But he still wasn't making much money. And money was more important than ever, because he and Zelma had long ago gotten over their shyness and were now very serious about each other. She often attended his performances and afterward they discussed how he had done. She usually had good ideas, but even when she didn't, Otis dug listening to her. She was the kind of chick he really liked: quiet but tough as nails when it came to something she believed in. After a few more months they were so serious that Otis asked her to marry him, and to no one's surprise she said yes, in spite of the fact that they were both only sixteen.

The biggest obstacle to setting a date for the wedding was money, and money came from working. Otis tried to hold down day jobs, but his singing always got in the way. For a while he worked as an attendant in a parking lot, but he got fired for singing in parked cars.

Then he worked as an orderly in Macon Hospital until he was fired for singing in the halls.

So he ended up spending a good deal of his time hanging around the "office" Phil had rented for his booking agency. There were lots of pictures of recording artists on the walls, so that when people came in they'd think Phil had a lot of clients. The office had a two-line phone with a "hold" button, and when a call came in Phil would answer, disguising his voice so he sounded like a girl. Then he'd ask the caller to hold because Mr. Walden was on the other line, and after a few minutes he'd come back on the phone using his own voice. He went through this routine so that callers would think a lot was going on at Walden Enterprises.

But both Phil and Otis knew there wasn't really much going on at all.

"Get any calls today?" Otis asked as he came into the office.

"Just one," Phil said, "and that was a wrong number."

"Man, bad news," Otis groaned, pulling a deck of cards out of his pocket.

Half an hour later Otis threw down his hand, leaned back in the chair, and stretched his long legs. "Say, isn't it about time for lunch?"

Phil was expecting that question. It seemed that more

and more often Otis just happened to be in the office at lunchtime.

"Yeah, I guess it is," he replied. "Why don't you get us four hot dogs and a couple of Cokes?" And he handed Otis two dollars.

When Otis returned, Phil asked him about the change.

"Oh, I spilled the Cokes, man," Otis said under his breath. "Had to go back and get two more."

This no-change business was happening more often, too, but Phil didn't say anything. He knew Otis was tight for money. And besides, Phil always beat Otis at blackjack.

About a week later, Otis came busting into the office. "Hey, man! Johnny has a lead on a three-night gig," Otis said, expecting Phil to start asking questions right away. But Phil just kept on looking out the window.

"You hear me, Phil? We might be getting a three-night gig," Otis repeated.

"Yeah, I heard you," Phil replied, turning around.

Otis saw that Phil looked worried, and the good news didn't seem to make him any happier.

"Let's play blackjack," Phil said, sounding tired.

"Okay, man, let's play." Otis shuffled the cards. "You know what we need? We need a lucky break," he said as he dealt the cards.

"Right, we need one of those breaks like you read

about in the papers. You know, where somebody in a big Cadillac with New York plates pulls up and says, 'Get in, kid. I'm going to make you a star,'" Phil said.

But he said it very glumly. Something was obviously bugging Phil but Otis thought he'd better cool it till Phil wanted to talk about it. However, when Otis had won the third hand in a row, he knew something was really wrong. Phil *never* lost at blackjack.

"Okay, Phil, let's have it, man. What's eating you? You didn't lose your job, did you?" Phil was working part time as a clerk in a men's clothing store.

"No, the job's not the problem. School's the problem," Phil replied, throwing down his cards. He was also a freshman at Mercer, a college in Macon.

"Oh, come on, man. You're not going to tell me you flunked something," Otis said. "I know you're too smart for that."

"No, grades aren't the problem either. Money's the problem. Tuition is due for the spring term and I'm sixty bucks short. I don't have it, there's no way to get it, and I can't stay in school without it."

Otis looked at Phil for a minute and then got up and walked out of the office without saying a word.

Three hours later he came back carrying a brown paper bag. He put it on the desk.

"What's that?" Phil asked.

"Take a look," Otis replied, sitting down and thumbing through a magazine.

Phil turned the sack upside down on his desk. Out poured the oldest, dirtiest pile of nickels, dimes, quarters, and crumpled-up dollar bills he'd ever seen. It looked like someone had been hoarding it for years.

"Otis, where'd you get this?" Phil asked, looking stunned.

"Don't worry about where it came from," Otis said, not looking up from the magazine. "Just make sure it's enough."

Phil counted it, and the stacks of change and the few bills amounted to $63.29.

Otis looked up. "Okay?" he asked.

"Otis, I can't take this money from you. Have you been saving it or did you borrow it or what?"

"Listen, man, like I told you, don't worry about how I got it. It was mine. I'm giving it to you. And that's that."

"But you need it worse than I do."

Otis looked at Phil with that look he got so often when he had to explain something he didn't think he should have to explain but had to anyway. Slowly he said, "You do the thinking for this outfit, right? Right. I do the singing and you do the thinking. And you really need an education. So you use the money to finish school."

"Thanks, Otis," Phil said in a subdued voice.

"I need a good manager. I got a good manager. And I'm gonna keep a good manager."

As Phil started putting the money back into the sack, Otis dropped the magazine on the desk, got up, and stretched.

"Hey, man, isn't it about time for dinner?"

Chapter 4

THE BIG BREAK

For the next few years, things didn't change much as far as Otis' career went—he and Johnny worked all the colleges, clubs, and concerts they could, but they hadn't made a record yet.

Otis and Zelma had gotten married in 1958, when they were just seventeen, and their son Dexter was born the following year. Otis really dug being a father, and was delighted when Zelma gave birth to a daughter, Carla, in 1962.

It was a big boost to their morale and their prospects when two music scouts heard and liked an instrumental guitar number that Johnny had written, "Soul Twist," and offered to foot the bill for Johnny to cut a demo record—that is, a record intended to show what an artist can do. Hopefully, a record company would buy the demo, give Johnny a contract, manufacture the record on its label, and distribute it.

So now—late in 1962—Johnny, Phil, and Otis were on their way, in a rented station wagon, to the Stax-Volt studios in Memphis.

"This is really a switch," Johnny said to Otis, who was at the wheel. "You driving me somewhere."

Otis pretended to be exasperated. "Johnny, you know if you or Phil tried to drive to this gig you'd be lucky to find your way out of Macon much less make it all the way to Memphis. Besides," he added, "you've got to keep your fingers loose for the recording session."

Phil and Johnny laughed—Otis was right about them being too nervous to drive. Besides, Otis wanted to see what a recording session was like and would have used any excuse to go along. Maybe, he thought, a promoter would offer him a break, too, someday.

No matter how much he'd thought about it—and he'd thought about it a lot, because Stax-Volt was *the* recording company for soul, the home of the "Memphis sound"—he wasn't ready for what he saw when they walked into the Stax-Volt studios on McLemore Street in Memphis.

The studios were in a run-down-looking former theater, which they entered through a rear door. There they were met by a pleasant receptionist who led them through a maze of windowless halls to the studio where the recording would be done. On their way they heard all kinds of sounds—typewriters, guitars, electronic thrums, drums, voices, snatches of music—and there was a general feeling of bustle and energy.

Otis didn't want to seem too much like a hick when he saw the studio, so he just kept quiet and stayed in the background, taking it all in. The place was full of floor mikes and boom mikes, with cables running everywhere, and some of the most authoritative-looking electronic equipment he'd ever seen. It was brightly lit, but it still seemed soulful, somehow, with various musicians sitting around checking out their instruments or running over parts of numbers and talking quietly to each other now and then, except for warm greetings whenever another musician would come in. The engineers were busy placing mikes and discussing the session with the musicians and the promoters, who were busy looking like Very Important People.

The back-up band Johnny was going to play with was also the backbone of the Stax-Volt operation as far as the company's overall sound went, a rhythm section that was—and still is—the best in the soul-music world, Booker T and the MG's: Booker T. Jones on piano and organ, Steve Cropper on guitar, Donald "Duck" Dunn on bass, and Al Jackson on drums. They'd made a hit, "Green Onions," that same year, and they worked together like they'd been destined for it. But each of them, in addition to playing on about 70 per cent of the records made by Stax-Volt artists and making their own records, wrote songs and were producers on many of the recordings of other groups for the company.

That was the rhythm section. The horns—saxes, trumpet, and trombone—were provided by a group known as the Mar-Keys, who were also regulars at Stax-Volt and tops in the R&B field.

Otis found a stool in a corner and sat down. From there he could look through the soundproof glass window into the control room. Now, that was really a gas —huge tape decks, control knobs and buttons, flashing lights, and a fellow with earphones—the recording engineer—signaling through the glass to the musicians before adjusting the controls.

Johnny and the MG's began to run through the numbers they were going to do—no big rush, they just kept going until they began to really feel where each other were at. When they took a break, Otis went out for coffee and sandwiches for everyone, but nobody paid much attention to him.

Finally the engineer switched on the intercom between the control room and the studio. His voice boomed through the speakers in the studio: "You fellows in there ready to cut one?"

"Yeah, let's go through it once and see how it sounds," Johnny replied.

"Okay, then, better come in here while we're recording," the engineer said to Otis.

That was fine with Otis, who wanted a closer look at the control room. He watched carefully as the engineer worked while Johnny and the band played. The sound that came out on the record depended almost as much on this man as it did on the musicians, he realized. The engineer could bring up one instrument or play down another. He was responsible for the overall balance and the particular emphasis different parts of a number got.

The group finished the number and waited for the engineer to rewind the tape for a playback. It was still the era of one-track monaural taping equipment, so if one guy made a mistake, it wasn't just a matter of redoing the track on which that instrument or voice was recorded—the entire group had to redo the number. Moreover, with only one track, everything on a record was recorded simultaneously, and there was no possibility of mixing in a tape of another performance with a live studio session or dubbing in some other effects. The extensive use of electronics in recording would have to await the development of multi-track recording equipment. Until then, except for volume techniques such as fade-outs and the engineer's adjustments, only what the musical artist was able to do in the studio ended up on the disc.

When the number was played back, nobody looked very happy. It just didn't sound right. Johnny said the horns were coming on too strong; Booker thought the engineer hadn't done a good job of balancing the bass. Another hour of playing and discussion went by without getting one good take.

Otis went out for coffee again. When he came back he handed a cup to Johnny.

"Man, if this ain't a mess," Johnny said, shaking his head.

There wasn't much for Otis to say. Everyone was standing around looking glum, and nobody was coming up with any new ideas.

"Let's forget it for today and try another session tomorrow," Jim Stewart, the owner of Stax-Volt, suggested.

"But we still have about forty minutes of studio time left on this session," objected Joe Galkin, one of the promoters.

Otis stopped playing with the rim of his paper coffee cup when he heard that. "Johnny," he said softly, "do you think Galkin would let me use the rest of the time to do a take?"

"I don't see why not," Johnny answered. "He's already paid for it."

Otis looked a little doubtful, but it was obvious he had the recording bug. All he needed was encouragement.

"Go on over and ask him," Johnny said firmly. "You know what they say: 'Nothing beats a failure but a try.' Besides, nothing ever kept you from asking for what you wanted before."

Otis put down his coffee. "Johnny, my man, you do have a point," he said with a smile.

Galkin, it turned out, was too discouraged to have any objections to Otis' suggestion. The musicians weren't too happy about starting all over again, but finally four of the eight men in the band said they'd stay.

As always, Otis was ready; it just so happened that he'd brought some of his arrangements along. The first number, "Hey, Hey, Baby," was a Little Richard standard that everyone in the band knew. The other, "These Arms of Mine," was a slow ballad Otis had written himself, but the arrangement was simple and the group picked it up in no time. In fifteen minutes both numbers were ready to be cut.

> These arms of mine feel so lonely,
> So lonely and so blue . . .

Otis wailed out the ballad slowly and deliberately, the tight energy of his voice rolling through the song even when he wasn't actually singing any lyrics. The taping went off without a hitch, but there wasn't much reaction from either Galkin or Stewart.

Then Otis launched into "Hey, Hey, Baby," a fast number, and came on just like Little Richard.

> Hey, hey, baby, you sure look fine.
> Every time I look at you, girl,
> You make me lose my mind.

This time, everyone in the studio paid attention.

When both numbers were completed, the engineer rewound the tape and signaled that the playback was ready. Otis couldn't believe his ears. That was *his* voice coming out with all that power! It was the first time he'd really heard himself sing. He started to smile and shake his head.

Otis wasn't the only one in the studio who couldn't believe it. As "Hey, Hey, Baby" played, Stewart and

Galkin looked at each other in obvious excitement. Little Richard had retired from singing to go into the ministry, and from the way this cut sounded, Otis Redding could very easily pick up the fans Richard had left behind.

When the playback was over, everybody was smiling. Galkin and Stewart wanted to talk with Phil and Otis right away about distributing the record, but Otis was still excited about hearing his voice.

"Can you play it back again?" he asked the engineer.

"Sure," he replied. "I'll play it as many times as you like."

Otis listened to the two numbers twelve times before Johnny could finally convince him it was time to leave.

"You sure got those promoters excited, Otis," Johnny commented as they walked out into McLemore Street.

"Yeah," Otis replied, becoming serious. "But that doesn't help you any."

"Well, it doesn't hurt, either. Don't worry about it. Tomorrow's another day. Some of that good luck'll rub off."

They both laughed.

"Did you hear that refrain on 'These Arms'?" Otis was still thinking about the recording session.

"Yeah, I heard it. Twelve times," Johnny replied with a smile.

Chapter 5

HIS OWN THING

Phil and Otis were sitting across from each other in the small office, a deck of cards between them, listening to Hamp Swann's show on the local soul-music station. They always listened to Swann, because he was ultra-hip—among other things, he'd been the first DJ in the country to play a James Brown record on the air. But since Otis' record had been released they listened avidly. So far, though, they hadn't heard "Hey, Hey, Baby" even once.

"Well," Otis sighed in the middle of the perpetual blackjack game he and Phil had going, "I guess we were wrong about everybody going for my Little Richard sound. That record's not doing a thing."

Phil picked up the cards and began dealing. "Look, Otis, it takes time—you know that. When a new record comes out by an unknown artist, it's hard to get the disc jockeys to play it. I mean, how many records do you think come in to a DJ each week?"

"Tons of 'em," Otis said.

"So okay," Phil went on. "It means the promoters have got to work twice as hard for an unknown, and those DJ's can be hard to convince. But that doesn't mean it won't happen. We've just got to be . . . Hey! Listen to that!"

What they were hearing was Otis' voice coming out of the radio, but it wasn't "Hey, Hey, Baby." It was "These Arms of Mine," his ballad.

"Well, I'll be damned," Otis said softly. "Who'd have thought they'd go for the flip side?"

And they did go for the flip side. "These Arms" received a good response. It started climbing on the regional soul charts. In two months it was number one in the area. It had taken eight months to happen, probably the longest "simmering" period a popular record had ever had, but it had made it.

Things began to move at Walden Enterprises. Otis began getting more offers for gigs, and sometimes both lines were busy with business calls. But Phil Walden couldn't be around to see Otis' career take off because he had to go into the Army for two years, and he was turning the booking agency over to his brother, Alan, until he got back.

There were a lot of things Phil and Otis had to talk over before Phil left. During one of these long discussions Phil said, "You know, Otis, the Little Richard thing was okay for the local audiences, but if you're going to make it really big, you'll have to develop your own style."

Otis nodded, deep in thought. He felt he had a unique way of putting a number across—the constant soul-charge that ran through "These Arms" was proof of it. Real success, and self-fulfillment, seemed to be in doing his own thing. On the other hand, he enjoyed doing his Little Richard routine; sounding like a famous and already successful star really made him feel good. But apparently, when it came to records at least, people liked Otis singing like Otis better than they liked him singing like someone else.

"Yeah, man," Otis finally replied. "You definitely have a point. I'm going to get it together. And when you get back, I'm going to be laying down a sound that nobody'll be able to imitate."

Otis believed that the music—the melody and the rhythm—was most important, that and the power of his voice. The lyrics really didn't make much difference. However, one point about lyrics was important: sing to the women. Otis sang to his female listeners, but in a way men could identify with, too. As Otis put it, "Get the women turned on to a song and they'll send the men out to buy the record."

He knew it would be easier to develop his own style if he used his own music, and by the time Stax-Volt was ready for him to do another recording session, in October 1963, he had enough material together for an album. When the people at Stax heard the ballad "Pain in My Heart," they knew they had a hit, and made it the title song for the album as well as releasing it as a single. And this time they were right from the beginning.

From then on, Alan Walden, who had taken over for his brother, had no trouble booking Otis. Most of his engagements were still in the "soul circuit," theaters and clubs across the South, as Otis had yet to make any appearances in the North, or to really catch on there with his recordings. Alan had been trying for a couple of months to get a booking at the Apollo Theater in New York City, but so far he hadn't been successful.

"Johnny, wouldn't it be cool if we got that Apollo gig?" Otis asked one night while the Pinetoppers were on their way home from a club date.

"That'd be great," Johnny replied, "as long as they weren't in any hurry for me to get there."

"What do you mean?" Otis asked.

"I'm not getting up in no plane, that's what I mean," Johnny answered, looking stubborn.

"Oh, come on, man, you must be kidding. You mean to tell me that if we had a chance to play the Apollo you wouldn't go?"

Johnny nodded. "That's right. Not if I had to fly."

Otis couldn't believe it. The Apollo was the temple of soul, and every R&B artist wanted to perform there. He could understand Johnny not wanting to fly if it wasn't really necessary—but if it came down to a choice between flying and not playing at the Apollo?

"I'm gonna make you a bet, Johnny," Otis said. "I bet you ten dollars that if that deal comes through you'll be right with me on that stage."

"You can make that bet if you want to," Johnny replied, "but that's ten bucks you might as well give me right now."

In May of 1964 the Apollo engagement finally did come through, but the deal wasn't exactly what Otis had hoped for.

"They'll only pay four hundred dollars for you, Otis, for a week's stint, and they won't bring up the band," Alan announced, not looking too happy. "I really tried to get them to raise the price, but they say you're hardly known up there, so that's the most they'll offer."

"Only four hundred! That'll hardly pay for transportation, much less anything else," Otis complained.

"Yeah, that's true," Alan agreed, "but it's a break anyway. The publicity and exposure in the North sure won't hurt, and you'll get a chance to do some heavy promoting on your new album."

"Well, the only way I'm going to make any bread on this gig is to take the bus," Otis said disgustedly.

"It's fifteen hours by bus, man," Alan exclaimed.

"It's fifteen hours but it's cheap," Otis said. And that was that.

Otis had thought he'd flip if the Apollo gig came through, but the thought of a fifteen-hour bus ride and then singing without Johnny put a damper on the whole deal.

"Hey, man, what about that bet?" Johnny asked when Otis told him the news.

"Well, we'll have to wait on the bet. After all, we never got a chance to see if you'd go or not."

Johnny laughed. "You're right. I wish we'd made a bet on whether or not *you* were going to fly."

Two weeks later Otis boarded the bus for New York. He wanted to look sharp when he hit the "Big Apple," so he was wearing his best—a shiny charcoal-brown suit, button-down-collar white shirt, and a brown paisley ascot. He knew he looked boss.

But he was totally unfamiliar with the hardships of long trips on buses. He hadn't thought of what fifteen hours could do to the collar of a shirt or the crease in a pair of pants. By the time the bus pulled into Richmond, Virginia, Otis looked and felt like he'd been through a battle with an octopus—and the octopus had won.

He changed buses in Richmond, and on the second bus he sat next to a girl reading an article on R&B in a soul magazine. Otis asked her about the R&B hits in the area.

"Have you heard 'Pain in My Heart'?" he asked.

"Sure," the girl replied. "It's been out in Richmond for a few weeks. I really dig Otis Redding."

"Well, I'm glad to hear that," Otis said with a big smile, "'cause that's what I want—people digging my sounds."

Otis waited for the reaction of joy and disbelief he expected this announcement to produce. The girl expressed disbelief all right, but it wasn't exactly the kind he'd expected.

"What do you mean, 'your sounds,'" she asked, a puzzled look on her face.

"Well, I guess it *is* my sound," Otis said. "I made the record."

"You're not trying to tell me *you're* Otis Redding?"

"The one and only."

At first the girl only smiled, then she burst out laughing. "You're really a gas," she giggled. "You looked so serious I almost believed you for a minute."

Otis didn't want to blow his cool by protesting too much, but that really hurt. "I'm telling you the truth," he insisted. "I'm Otis Redding and I'm on my way to New York for a gig at the Apollo."

The girl stopped smiling. In fact, she looked just a little bit angry. "Oh, come on. You must think I'm stupid. From the way he sounds on his records, I know Otis Redding must be sharp, always dap. He wouldn't be going around in wilted shirt collars and crumpled-up pants. Besides," she concluded as she picked up her magazine, "would Otis Redding be riding a *bus* to New York? You've got to be kidding."

Otis slumped back in his seat, folded his arms, and glared out the window. He was mad, and he made up his mind right then—he wasn't ever going to ride a bus anywhere again, not even from New York back to Macon. From now on, if he couldn't either drive or fly to a gig, then he wouldn't take it.

But it was worth it, even on the bus, to make it to New York and the Apollo. Many people have tried to describe what the Apollo means to black music and to the black community, and Otis felt it all when he first entered the aging theater on 125th Street in the heart of Harlem. It may have been funky, but it was alive with memories of the past from the great days of vaudeville through the heyday of the 1930's and 40's, and it was still alive with soul in the 60's.

And he *had* to feel a little nervous about appearing before that audience for the first time—everybody knew that if they liked you they'd really let you know it, but if they *didn't* like you they'd let you know that, too—hissing and booing and practically driving you off the stage.

But Otis didn't need to worry. They liked him fine, and although he'd been sure he couldn't really do his very best without Johnny, it turned out the Apollo house band was totally flexible, full of real pros, and Otis felt right at home after a few rehearsals. By the end of the week he felt like he'd been born on that stage.

Even so, in spite of the good reception and some valuable contacts he made in New York, the doors didn't suddenly open in the North. So Otis and Johnny continued to work on their home ground, the South. But staying in the South was not always without problems.

The audience screamed its approval as Otis Redding, headliner of the show, danced off the stage and the lights came up for intermission.

"Man, I thought that balcony was going to fall down, the way those folks were rocking up there," Otis said as he and Johnny entered one of the backstage dressing rooms.

"Yeah, and the people downstairs weren't doing so bad either," Johnny added.

The group was performing for a segregated audience that night, which meant that blacks sat in the balcony and whites downstairs.

Both Otis and Johnny turned when they heard somebody at the door, and saw two white men standing there.

"Jus' wanted to tell y'all that you niggers can sure sing," one of them slurred as he leaned against the doorway. They were obviously drunk.

"I seen a lot of nigger bands before," the other man said, "but you boys are the best nigger band I ever heard."

Otis looked at Johnny and saw that his face was hard as stone. Johnny was getting ready to say something but Otis put his hand on Johnny's arm, signaling him to keep quiet.

"Yeah, you boys play all right for niggers," the first man echoed as they stumbled down the hall.

Otis got up and closed the door.

"Why didn't you let me tell those rednecks off?" Johnny demanded.

"What good would that do?" Otis asked. "What they say doesn't mean a thing. They're only sounding stupid —we don't have to stoop to *their* level. As a matter of fact, those guys are helping us make our living by paying to come and see us. So who cares if they make jackasses out of themselves?"

Johnny still couldn't buy it. "Sure, Otis, but how can your pride take it?"

"My pride comes from my soul, what I am and what I do," Otis replied, "not from what some ignorant drunk does or doesn't think about me. Man, I can't be bothered with that."

Johnny stood in the middle of the floor for a long while, and neither he nor Otis said anything.

Suddenly he looked at his watch. "Come on, man," he said, grabbing his jacket. "Let's go out there and share some of that soul with our brothers in the balcony."

Chapter 6

THE BEST-LAID PLANS

"Here is Redding's blood and guts, and anyone who hears *Dictionary of Soul* recognizes its greatness instantly."

That's what rock critic Jon Landau had to say about the album that he and many others feel is the high spot in Otis' recording career—*Dictionary of Soul*, made in 1964 and released early in 1965.

By this time, Otis had formed his close relationship with Booker T and the MG's, and particularly with guitarist Steve Cropper, who was the producer on many of Otis' Stax-Volt albums and with whom Otis collaborated on a number of tunes.

Steve, whose background was in country and western music, had taught himself electronics and sound engineering by working at the Stax-Volt studios from its earliest days. He liked working with Otis as much as Otis liked working with him—the vibrations were always good. As Steve has said, "I'm satisfied with everything I ever did on Otis' records. Everything he did was an accomplishment—what he put on it made the whole thing. It was Otis and it sounded great."

One of the Redding-Cropper collaborations, "Fa Fa Fa Fa Fa (Sad Song)," was first recorded on the *Dictionary* album; it's a charming, completely relaxed number you can't get out of your head once you've heard it. And Otis continued to do his searing ballads, especially "You're Still My Baby" and "Try a Little Tenderness." That song, which Frank Sinatra had made famous many years earlier, is astounding when Otis does it, starting out slowly, almost painfully, and then working into a "sock it to me" finish that leaves the listener gasping.

He did the Beatles' "Day Tripper" in a very Memphis way, giving it new life. Other "standard" songs—"Sweet Lorraine" and "Tennessee Waltz"—also got new life in the Redding manner on the *Dictionary* album. And he also did the blues, and his own up-tempo pure soul things. He did it all.

Otis could have adapted his singing to a less rugged, more "refined" style to try to reach the wider white audience that—in 1965, anyway—was not hip to the raw simplicity of rhythm and blues. He wanted to reach that audience. But he didn't change his style. *Dictionary of*

Soul is proof of that, with its strength and simplicity. For the time being, he had to sing the way he sang— he'd started with Little Richard and a heritage of gospel music and he'd worked it into his own unique sound, and that's where it was at for him.

Not that he sang the same way on all his numbers. He had a wide emotional range, but it was always that Redding sound, that intensity, that made you know it was Otis singing, Otis being Otis and doing what he did best, as he'd known all along he would do.

If white America wasn't ready for Otis yet, black audiences certainly were—*Dictionary* was a big hit with them. And Stax-Volt knew they had a good thing going, so they decided to cash in on the popularity by putting together a show of regular Stax performers, with Otis as the headliner, to do a series of one-night engagements throughout the South.

It was a hard schedule, the kind that many R&B and jazz artists have had to live through—thirty days on the road, a long show nearly every night, into and out of planes and cars and buses, into and out of a series of nameless hotels, never quite sure what city you're in on a particular night. But the audiences were there in every city, and that's what it was all about—the performers who gave, and the audiences who received, and who received so much they gave something back to the performers: enthusiasm, love, inspiration, soul-power.

Otis was a hard-driving man; he thrived on this kind of interaction. And he never stopped working. "Even when he was on the road," Steve Cropper said, "he'd be in a hotel or on the bus with a guitar in his hands, working on ideas."

When the tour was over, box-office receipts totaled $250,000, which, as Otis, Stax-Volt, and Alan Walden agreed, was a good thing. So they quickly arranged another thirty-day tour, and they did it all over again—only better.

"Hey, man, you arrived just in time," Alan said as Otis came into the office one afternoon shortly after the second tour.

"Hope I'm in time for somethin' good, 'cause I sure don't need nothin' bad," Otis replied as he sat down.

"It's good, all right," Alan said. "I just finished talking to the people in Memphis."

Otis' face became serious, as it always did when they discussed anything about his career.

Alan continued. "They just added up the receipts for the second tour, and it comes to five hundred thousand."

"Come again?" Otis almost whispered.

"Five hundred thousand," Alan repeated, pronouncing each figure slowly and carefully.

"In thirty days!"

"Exactly double what you brought in before."

"Wow!" Otis leaned back in his chair. "That must be some kind of record."

And, as it turned out, it was. The Otis Redding/Stax-Volt revue had brought in the largest amount of box-office receipts ever received by any R&B tour.

There was a new member on Otis' staff—one of Claude Sims's brothers, Earl Sims, who was road manager. Otis had a special place in his heart for the Sims family, and for the fact that Claude had given him his first professional gig when he'd been too young to *be* in a nightclub, much less perform in one. Earl fit right in—he was bouncy and cheerful and loyal and always worked fast. That's how he got the nickname Speedo.

Being a road manager was hard work—it meant coordinating everything about out-of-town appearances, making sure that everyone was on time, that hotel arrangements were set, that transportation was settled, that all the equipment and instruments were working and in place at the auditorium or club where the group was appearing. But another part of Speedo's job was just to pay attention to all the details during actual performances, and he got to know Otis' moods as well as anyone ever did, just by looking.

But one evening Speedo couldn't understand what was bugging Otis. It was obvious the big man wasn't satisfied, even though the show had gone off without a hitch. The theater had good equipment and Otis' voice had traveled loud and clear. Johnny Jenkins had done his usual beautiful thing on the guitar, working with Steve Cropper of the MG's, and the Mar-Keys had been right in there, too. No doubt about it, it had been a strong performance. No doubt, either, that Otis had that certain look on his face when he came off the stage after his last number, the look that meant he was upset about something.

Speedo had coffee ready when Otis got to the dressing room.

"Otis, how come you're looking so down in the mouth?" Speedo asked as he handed Otis a cup of coffee.

"That show just didn't come off like it should have," Otis said dejectedly.

"What do you mean, man? It sounded great."

"No," Otis answered flatly. "I didn't get the feeling that the audience was really swinging with me. You know, like I wasn't reaching them."

"I don't think it had anything to do with you," Speedo

protested. "*You* were fine! Maybe they were sort of a dead bunch of folks. Sometimes it's like that."

"That may be," Otis replied, "but I should have been able to get them going anyway. Getting the audience involved is important—that's why we're out there."

This was true. Grooving with the audience was Otis' specialty; in fact, it was the most important part of his in-person style. He'd sing and dance and shout and just plain carry on till he got everybody in the place clapping and swaying. The Otis Redding style was a total experience. It wasn't enough for the music just to sound good. It had to *feel* good.

Otis flopped into a chair just as Johnny, the Mar-Keys, and some of Otis' buddies from Macon came in.

"What's wrong?" Johnny asked right away.

"Yeah, man," one of the other musicians added. "You look like you just lost your last friend."

"Otis doesn't feel right about the way the audience responded tonight," Speedo explained.

"I don't know how he *feels*, but he sure *looks* pitiful," Ronnie, one of the Mar-Keys, teased.

"C'mon, Otis. Let's make it to the party," Speedo suggested. "Maybe it'll cheer you up."

Everyone else at the party, an after-show affair given by one of the other acts, soon was grooving, but Otis spent the entire night sitting alone. When the group returned to their hotel early in the morning, happily tired out, Otis was still stomping around, complaining about the shortcomings of their act. But in the middle of it all, a song started noodling around in his head.

Ronnie, slouched on the sofa, opened a sleepy eye. "Poor ol' Otis. You look so sad. You oughtta write a song called 'Mr. Pitiful.'"

"Man, you might just have something there," Otis said, reaching for his faithful pad and pencil. "What I'm feeling sure *is* pitiful."

After scribbling a few notes, Otis asked Speedo where Steve Cropper was.

"He's on the next floor," Speedo replied. "Why? You want him *now?* It's after four, and he didn't go to the party."

"Yeah—get him, will you? I got to get this song out of my head, and I know Steve can help."

Otis had his guitar out before Speedo got to the door, and by the time he came back with a sleepy Steve, Otis was well into it.

"Hey, man—this better turn out to be the biggest hit you ever had," Steve said. "I was really out there. Let's hear what you got."

Speedo got some coffee going and then he and the

others left. Otis and Steve worked, in their quiet way, until around seven-thirty in the morning. "Mr. Pitiful" was born, and it did turn out to be a big hit. And for a while after that, everyone called Otis "Mr. Pitiful."

Songwriter, recording artist, electrifying performer —Otis Redding was all of them now, and doing well. Things could still go wrong, though. Like one night in Roanoke, Virginia.

"Now, where can that fool be?" Speedo muttered as he stopped pacing the floor of the dressing room long enough to light another cigarette. Otis and most of the Mar-Keys were there, all looking glum.

"What time we supposed to start?" Otis asked.

"Nine, and it's quarter of now," Speedo replied.

"Man, if this ain't a mess," Ronnie said, from his seat in the corner.

"They've really been promoting the show up here— this place is sold out. There's gonna be a mighty mad bunch of people out there if we go on without a drummer," said Phalon, one of the Mar-Keys.

"Hey, will you all keep quiet for a minute?" Speedo snapped. "I've got to think."

Speedo was thinking all right, and thinking hard. As road manager, he was responsible for making sure that things like this didn't happen. And when they did, he was the one who had to straighten them out—like finding a drummer out of no place at the last possible minute.

Otis finished adjusting his tie and got up from the dressing table. "What time is it now?" he asked.

"Ten of," Ronnie answered.

"Okay. Let's go out and check the setup on the stage."

"Otis, what're you gonna do?" Speedo ground out his cigarette, looking bewildered. "You seem to forget that we don't have a drummer."

"*You* seem to forget that I've been wailin' on drums since I was thirteen," Otis replied.

"But how're you gonna play the drums and do your act at the same time?"

"I used to do it when I had to. Guess I have to now," said Otis, heading for the stage.

Speedo shook his head. He'd worked as manager for other groups and knew how it was—as soon as somebody became a headliner he wouldn't do anything but his own act. Those guys felt that pinch-hitting for someone else lowered their image. If something went wrong, it was up to the road manager to fix it, and that was that. But here was Otis, more than willing to sit in for the missing drummer. He was something else.

The back-up band for the show was a large one, twenty pieces, including the Mar-Keys. Otis and Speedo worked with the musicians and stagehands to rearrange the placement of the instruments, and the drums were brought down front. Usually Otis held the mike in one hand while performing; now the mike was put on a stand at one side of the drums. Otis sat down to see how the setup would work, but he didn't like it because he didn't have enough room to move and wouldn't be able to see the audience clearly.

"Think we can lower the overhead mike?" he asked.

"Sure," a stagehand replied.

"I hope he makes it quick," Speedo commented, looking at his watch. "We're fifteen minutes late already."

When the mike was lowered and the other one removed, Otis sat down behind the drums again.

"How's it now?" Speedo asked.

"Okay," Otis replied. "Let's hit."

The master of ceremonies looked relieved when Speedo gave him the signal; the crowd was getting restless. Strutting on stage, the MC announced that Otis Redding was not only going to sing, but would also play the drums. The place broke up, and by the time the curtain opened, the theater was alive with cheering and whistles.

Otis really tore into the drums. His whole body moved and shook with the best. Speedo stood backstage, fingers snapping and toes tapping. Not only had Otis saved the show, but the audience was getting double their money's worth tonight.

By now 90 per cent of Otis Redding's life was public, a continuous merry-go-round of personal appearances, recording, business arrangements. The other 10 per cent of his life was personal, with Zelma and the children, of whom there were now three. In addition to Dexter, who was six, and Carla, three, there was now Otis III, born the previous year, to carry on the name.

Otis was rising fast. But he had learned some lessons through the years. To get to the top and stay there meant he must keep on working, and working hard. The top was still a long climb ahead, so he couldn't just settle down. So far, he was still only part of what was called the "chitlin' circuit," playing in small nightclubs or city auditoriums, mostly in the South. Furthermore, although his records were very popular on soul stations, they weren't being played on the "Top Ten" stations.

Otis loved performing, no matter where or for whom. But he knew that if he was really going to make it big he was going to have to move into the so-called "legitimate" music circles. He was going to have to land jobs at name nightclubs. And his records were going to have to be played everywhere, so everybody could hear them.

It wasn't going to be easy. For all his planning, Otis wasn't sure just how he was going to do it.

Chapter 7

A NEW HOME, AN OLD FRIEND

Maybe Otis was still not as widely recognized as he'd planned to be by this time—even though he was only twenty-four years old—but he was doing all right.

"Honey, do you know we're practically rich?"

Otis was sitting with Zelma, watching Dexter and Carla playing with the new tricycle he'd just brought home.

"I mean it," he continued when Zelma looked up. "All these tours and albums are making a lot of money, even after taxes. And what have we got to show for it?"

"What are you driving at, Otis? You sound like you've got something on your mind."

Otis nodded. "I sure do. I got a house on my mind. In fact, not a house, a ranch. Yes, sir, a real spread."

"You're crazy, Otis Redding," Zelma told him. "You're no Texas cowboy."

"Don't aim to be. Don't you remember, 'way back

79

when, when I talked about having a ranch? Well, we can really do it now. Right here outside of Macon in the good old state of Georgia."

It was the beginning of a dream come true when Otis bought his 300-acre ranch a few miles outside of Macon in the summer of 1965. Only a few additions were needed for it to fit exactly the image that Otis had always had of the way he wanted his home to be—a 300,000-gallon swimming pool and a pasture stocked with prize cattle and several prize horses. But most important, a large, comfortable brick house was built on the land—the new home for Otis' parents.

Reverend Redding hadn't relented completely about Otis' career—he still didn't approve of his son singing in "sinful" nightclubs. Even so, he had long ago realized that Otis was doing what Otis had to do, and was doing it better than anyone else. And it was obvious that however hectic Otis' career was, he was still a decent, beautiful person and hadn't been corrupted. Although he was quiet about it, Reverend Redding *was* proud of his son. Otis' prediction had come true.

"Hey, Otis! Get your clothes on, man, so we can go fix that fence," Speedo said as he crossed the lawn.

"I'd forgotten all about it."

"Time to stop forgetting, 'cause I came out here to help and that's what I plan to do."

Actually, Speedo liked working around the ranch. Often one could find all the boys in the group out at the Big O, as the ranch was called, mending a fence or painting a barn or just enjoying being out in the country.

Otis and Speedo worked through the afternoon.

"What do you say we take the horses out for a ride?" Otis suggested when they had finished fixing the fence.

"I knew you were going to say that," Speedo groaned. "You must think you're a cowboy or something. Every chance you get, you want to be up on a horse."

Speedo was right. Otis loved horses, and now that he had his own, he rode whenever he was home.

"C'mon, man," Otis said with a laugh. "Let's play cowboys."

"But, Otis, you know what happens to me every time I get on a horse," Speedo complained.

"Let me see." Otis walked slowly around Speedo, pretending to examine him closely. "No, man—your pants won't split this time."

"Okay," Speedo said, "but if they do, that's it. I ain't riding *no* more."

Otis and Speedo went to the stable and saddled the horses. Otis mounted easily, and then turned to look down at Speedo. "Well, what're you waiting for?"

"Here goes," Speedo announced, hoisting himself up in the saddle. Everything stayed in one piece. "So far, so good."

Otis laughed as they moved out of the stable.

No matter how many times he rode around the Big O, Otis was always excited by what he saw. Tall Georgia pines whispered around him, and the air was full of the smells and sounds of the out-of-doors.

Suddenly there was the sound of something else—something tearing.

"I'll be doggone," Speedo shouted. "I told you, Otis, I told you!" He got down from his horse and began to examine the rip in his pants.

"Speedo, you must be doing something wrong," Otis laughed.

"That may be," Speedo replied, "but whatever it is, I'm only gonna do it just long enough to get back to the house. And then that's it for me and horses."

Otis didn't spend all his time "playing cowboy" when he was in Macon. He also spent time writing music and working on the affairs of Walco Music Company, a music-publishing and production firm he had founded.

To Otis, Walco was the most important thing he was doing, because it provided a solid financial base under the earnings of his performing career. Through it he kept control of his compositions, which meant that he was sure to receive royalties for his songs, not only when he performed them or recorded them, but when anyone else did. Also, Walco served as a center for the discovery and development of local Macon talent. Otis remembered how hard it had been for him to start out in the music world—and how lucky he'd been—and he was always on the lookout to help a good unknown performer make a start.

One of his finds was eighteen-year-old Arthur Conley, who had been singing with a group called the Corvettes. Otis wrote a song for him. "Sweet Soul Music," and Arthur recorded it for Stax-Volt. The next thing they knew, it was a million-seller and Arthur Conley was on the way up.

But Otis didn't let Arthur coast along on his success; he urged him to keep working at his singing and his delivery. Arthur did, and he is very grateful to Otis Redding. "I want the world to know how much I loved and admired Otis," Arthur has said. "And I want to try and follow in his footsteps by trying to help others, like he helped me." Otis had that kind of an impact on the people he worked with and helped.

In 1965 he wrote a rocking number called "Respect" and published it through Walco. He sang it often—it's the highlight of a number of his albums—but it wasn't until 1967, when Aretha Franklin recorded it, that it became a gold-record million-seller. And the royalties keep coming in to Walco Music.

It was apparent that Otis was quite a businessman. But this didn't detract from his other talent, that of performing both "live" and on records. Although Otis himself never released a million-seller during his performing career, every one of his records sold over 150,000 copies, about the most any disc could do in the soul market. As a matter of fact, "These Arms of Mine," his first single, was still selling strong three years after its release.

Coming back home always made Otis feel good. He had his family, his ranch, and his business. And he had a chance to work with Johnny Jenkins again.

Now that Otis was getting bookings nearly every night, most of them not near Macon, he and his band simply had to fly to their gigs if they were to make them on time. And Johnny had meant it when he said he wouldn't fly, so he and Otis could get together only when Otis was playing in the Macon area.

"Well, Johnny, you ready to split?" Otis asked early one morning after a gig he and Johnny had done together in Macon.

"Yeah, man, I'm ready to make it," Johnny responded.

Johnny and Otis said good-by to the few band members and their friends who were still talking in front of the club and then crossed the street to Otis' car. Johnny chuckled as he slid into the bucket set.

"Sure beats the old Buick," he said.

"You said it," Otis answered. "What a heap *that* was."

Otis didn't start the motor right away. Instead, he and Johnny sat there, listening to the sounds of the night and thinking. That's how it always was now that Johnny and Otis didn't see each other as often as they used to. After any show they did together they'd sit in the car and talk.

Otis lit a cigarette and watched the smoke curl up and drift out the window. Leaning his head back against the seat, he thought about the performance he and Johnny had just given.

"It was a groove doin' those old numbers again. Some of the cats really broke up when we cut into 'Hey, Hey, Baby.'"

"You ain't kiddin'," Johnny replied. "You know, some of those people were around when we were doing those numbers together as kids. They remember how we sounded then, and it really shook them up to see that after all these years you and I can still get the same vitality going."

Otis smiled. "It shakes me up a little, too. Your guitar

sound is still just natural for my singing. Nothing's changed. I still need your sound in the show."

Johnny leaned forward, propped his elbows on his knees, and rested his head in his hands.

"Otis, I know what you're leading up to. We've been through it a dozen times before. I'd really dig joining the group on a permanent basis, but I'm just *not* going to fly. Period. I'll gig with you anywhere within driving distance of Macon, but farther than that, I can't do it."

It was true that he and Johnny had been through this before, but Otis really wanted Johnny in his group. He wanted him as a friend and he wanted him as a performer. And Otis Redding could be very persistent when it came to things he wanted.

Both men remained silent for several minutes. Then Otis thought of a new line of persuasion.

"Hey, Johnny, remember the dance we played for that white fraternity about six years ago?"

"How could I forget that one?" Johnny replied with a grin.

"Boy, you really cussed when it was fifteen minutes after we were supposed to start and the rest of the band hadn't shown up yet."

Johnny laughed. "Naturally, they'd broken down in the Buick."

"Again," Otis added.

"Yeah, again. Boy, that car was a mess. It was just luck that you and I had another car that night and some of the instruments."

"How about the look on the social chairman's face when he saw just the two of us up there, you tuning your guitar and me setting up the drums?" Otis asked.

Johnny burst out laughing again. "Yeah, but what really knocked me out was the straight look on your face when you told him we were ready to start." Johnny was laughing so hard now he could hardly get the words out.

"When the poor guy asked where the rest of the group was," Otis gasped, "we told him that his fraternity was in for a special feature of our act—the greatest two-piece band in the land!"

"He may not have believed what he saw, but he sure believed what he heard."

"Man! Did we sound good together that night. Just the two of us playing and singing. We really did rock."

Johnny leaned back in his seat. His eyes were a little moist from all the laughing, but they also had a faraway look, a look they got when he was remembering something good from the past.

"Yeah," he said softly. "We were really close that night."

"Johnny," Otis began seriously, "we could be gigging like that again. We could be playing together every night. And you know we sound good. The Mar-Keys on the horns, Al Jackson doing his thing on the drums, and you and Stevie Cropper pouring it out on guitar. Man, nothing could stop us."

Johnny was listening carefully to what Otis was saying. Maybe this time he'll give in, Otis thought.

"Besides," Otis went on, "I promised you a long time ago that if I made it, you'd make it. I want to keep that promise."

Johnny sat and thought. "There's nothing I'd like better than to be working with you, Otis," he said finally. "But this thing I have about flying—well, it's kind of a belief. I just don't think that God meant for me to fly. Maybe my belief will change. I don't think it will, but if it does, you better believe that you'll be the first one to hear about it. Right now, though, there's nothing else I can say."

Otis looked at his friend. It was hard for him to get used to the fact that, the way things stood, the more successful he became, the less chance he'd have to play with Johnny. That made him really sad, but he respected Johnny's feelings.

"Okay, man," Otis said softly. "I understand. I tell you what—since I may not be able to keep my promise about bringing you all the way to the top with me, I'll make a promise that I won't bug you any more about flying."

After Otis dropped Johnny off at his home, he continued to think about flying as he drove out to the ranch.

Otis liked flying. Sometimes he was annoyed by long waits in airports, and he didn't much like flights scheduled at odd hours, but he really enjoyed flying itself. What he'd *really* like to do, he thought, was get his own small plane, and then learn how to fly it himself. That would be a gas. Maybe someday . . .

Chapter 8

GETTIN' IT TOGETHER

All of a sudden, it seemed, Phil Walden was back from the service. Well, not all of a sudden—a lot of things had happened in the two years he'd been gone—but now here he was, rarin' to go.

Otis was happy to have Phil back, both as a business manager and a friend. With both Phil and Alan Walden working on the business end of things, and Speedo as road manager, Otis felt that his career was about to break loose in a big way.

"Looks like things started popping after I left," Phil said jokingly.

"They may have been moving fast before, but they're really gonna roll now that we're all working together again," Otis responded.

"I can't wait to see good ol' Rockin' Otis Redding on the stage tonight," Phil said.

Phil had been able to keep up with Otis' recordings

while he was gone, but it had been a long time since he'd seen Otis perform in person. And that, of course, was what Otis Redding was all about.

"You'll see me tonight," Otis said, "but it won't be the ol' Rockhouse you remember. You think I got my singing thing together? Man, that's only what you can hear on those records. Wait till you see what I'm doing now with my act."

"Okay, Otis," Phil laughed. "You go right on bragging. But just keep in mind that I'm gonna be listening to every sound and watching every move you make, and I know you from 'way back when. You'll never hear the end of it if you mess up."

Otis laughed along with him. "Phil," he said, "tonight you're gonna see the best entertainment you've *ever* seen, if I do say so myself."

Otis could be pretty sure his prediction would be correct. After all, he'd done a lot of shows since Phil had left and he and the group were always polishing their act. And 99 per cent of the time, everything went off as they had planned. Otis' determination to get his act exactly right was paying off.

The show that night started off with a bang, with Sam Cooke's "Shake," which Otis did all the time, especially since Sam's death in 1964. The audience was really alive, and responded to Otis' hard-driving singing. It was his kind of audience, and he served up the numbers with the power of a steam shovel. In between numbers he kept up a dialogue with the crowd that got them clapping and calling for more. Continuous energy —that was the secret behind the Otis Redding sound. He dished out energy in great heaps and always seemed to have plenty to spare.

The last number of the show was "Respect." The way they had rehearsed it, Otis was to cut from the verse back to the chorus at the end of the number, repeat the chorus three times, then cut sharply back to another round of the verse just as the audience would be thinking the number was going to end. Then the group would move to the big buildup, a technique that had become one of the trademarks of the Redding style.

The procedure wasn't complicated—with Otis it never was—but it did mean that he and the group had to stay together through the cues for shifting from chorus to verse and back again. But that was no problem.

Otis started out:

> What you want, you know I got it.
> What you need, baby, you know I got it.

The group jammed on with a steady beat. The audience was totally caught up in the number, clapping along.

Otis went through the verse once, then launched into the chorus, making it seem that he was wrapping up the number:

R-E-S-P-E-C-T, tell you what it means to me.
R-E-S-P-E-CT, take care, TCB.

Steve Cropper hit the series of chords that were the signal for Otis to cut back to the verse, and suddenly Otis realized he couldn't remember the words! There he was in the middle of the stage, in front of fifteen hundred people, and he'd forgotten the words of a song he'd written himself.

But the Redding energy carried him through. He just kept right on singing, simply filling in with sounds: "Na-na-na, ta-ta-ta." He completely suspended the rhythm the group had been playing and started to improvise around the most soulful sounds the audience had ever heard: "Lord have mercy, respect, ah-ah-ah . . ."

The band faded out and only drummer Al Jackson kept a light beat for Otis' new thing. He was really getting into it now, and he rocked along for as long as he felt like it—and as long as it took him to remember the words.

When he was ready to cut back into the song, he

dropped his hand sharply down to his side, hoping the band would catch the signal. It did, and the whole group swung back into, "What you need, you know I got it." It was really beautiful.

When the number was over the crowd went wild, rushing the stage. Phil was beaming as he greeted Otis when he finally came off.

"Man, you said you were gonna create your own thing, but that was too much. I've never heard *anybody* bring off a number like that before!"

Otis was grinning. "Until tonight, I never heard a number like that before either."

Phil looked puzzled, and Otis, laughing, explained what had happened. "I tell you," he said, "it didn't seem funny for a minute there. But it turned out all right. I think maybe I've hit on a good new technique to use in my act."

"You sure have," Phil grinned. "See what my coming back has done already? First thing out you forget the words and then come up with a whole new thing."

"Yeah. Welcome back, Phil," Otis said. "Welcome back."

For the rest of 1965 and all through 1966 Otis kept working hard, recording regularly for Stax-Volt and continuing to tour, both with a Stax package show and on his own. The rest of the country—outside of the South and the black communities of the North—was just beginning to become aware that soul music was the inspiration for much of the music that many of the most popular white rock and roll groups were doing.

The Beatles, for example, revealed that they were influenced not only by Elvis Presley (who himself had been influenced by black artists in the 1950's), but by American blues singers. The Rolling Stones openly admitted their debt to the music of black America, and admired Otis Redding in particular. They recorded several of his tunes. Otis repaid their compliment by doing the Mick Jagger-Keith Richards tune "Satisfaction"—which was natural, because Jagger and Richards said they'd been influenced to write the song in the first place by the kind of music Otis had always sung and heard.

So, by way of messengers from England, came the word that most Americans were overlooking the source of their English idols' inspiration—the soul music of black America, the raucous, vibrating, wailing sound of the blues. James Brown was bigger than ever; B. B. King began to receive some long-overdue recognition; Ike and Tina Turner were being heard more often by white audiences, as well as black; Ray Charles was reaching *everybody*; Aretha Franklin was paying her dues and getting ready to make it big. So was Otis. He still hadn't broken into the "Top Ten," but he was on his way, and still growing.

Among Otis' special friends in the R&B world was Carla Thomas, who also recorded for Stax-Volt and often appeared with Otis in shows sponsored by the recording company.

Someone at Stax suggested that Otis and Carla team up on a record. Otis had never thought about working as a duet before, but he liked Carla's sound and understood the way she approached her singing, so they agreed to cut a single together.

When "Tramp" was released, it immediately began to soar on the R&B charts. Encouraged by the success, Otis and Carla began working together on an album. They lived up to the title of the album, *King and Queen of Soul*, in their performance on the disc, and soon fans began referring to them by their new titles. Stax-Volt and Walco Music Company even received letters addressed simply to "The King and Queen."

Attracted by the great popularity of the album, a black newspaper, the Chicago *Daily Defender*, decided to honor the "royal" couple by featuring them as special guests of the annual Billiken Day parade in late 1966. At the end of the parade, there would be a ceremony to crown Otis and Carla officially as the King and Queen of Soul.

Otis was pleased about the honor, and he looked forward to taking part in the parade and greeting his fans. But there was another reason why he was happy about the trip: his transportation to Chicago would be provided by his own private plane, and it would be his first trip in it.

Because Otis had to travel so much, he had decided that a private plane was the only solution to crowded air terminals and long delays. That way, he could set his own schedules and make his own travel arrangements.

Otis had the plane, a Beechcraft, custom fitted especially for his needs, and by the time it was ready it cost $200,000. He hired Dick Frazier, a veteran pilot, to handle the craft and teach him how to fly.

When the plane lifted off the runway at Macon for the trip to Chicago, Otis was itching with things he wanted to ask. He watched Dick closely for a while, and then began to bombard him with questions.

Dick laughed. "Hold on, Otis. You're not going to be able to learn it all in one trip."

The glistening new craft was a beautiful sight as it landed in Chicago. Otis stepped out first, as soon as the plane stopped, expecting that some members of the press would be there for pictures. Flashbulbs started popping when he appeared, but not all of the cameras belonged to professional photographers. Hundreds of Redding fans had come out to greet the "King."

Otis had never been more proud. Here he was, stepping out of his own plane, being heartily cheered by his fans, and about to be crowned the King of Soul.

When he returned to Macon, Otis stopped by at The Pines, one of his favorite hangouts. As usual on a Saturday, the place was full of regulars, guys who had grown up in Macon and had known each other since childhood.

"Hey, how ya doin'?" The greetings rang out as Otis came in the door.

"Fine—what's happenin'?" Otis smiled back as he slapped a few palms. All of these black faces were familiar—friends from grammar school, high school, and church. Some of these men were making a fairly decent living by running small grocery stores, shoeshine parlors, and the like, but most of them were in menial jobs such as busboy and hospital attendant. It didn't make any difference to Otis what his friends wore or what kind of jobs they had—except that he wished they could do better, of course. If he could have, he would have changed things, and maybe, in some small way, he might be able to help if he made it really big.

"Set everybody up on me, Carl," Otis told the bartender.

"Any time," Carl replied with a grin. "Oh, by the way. See that older guy sitting over in the corner there? He'd like to talk to you."

"What does he want?"

"'Fraid I don't know—I just told him you'd probably be in sometime today, and here you are."

Otis made his way through the crowd to the booth where the man was sitting.

"Hello, I'm Otis Redding. Did you want to talk to me?"

"Yes, yes. I recognize you now. You're Reverend Redding's boy. My name is Ed Carter. The last time I saw you, you were just a half-pint." Otis smiled as he lowered his six-foot frame into the booth opposite Mr. Carter.

"Guess I have grown a little," Otis said. "What's on your mind, Mr. Carter?"

"Well," Mr. Carter replied, fussing with some papers he had on the table, "it's about my grandchildren. You see, Mrs. Carter and I have raised them since they were just little tads. They're good kids, bright kids. Both of them go to the local high school—the same school you went to."

Otis nodded.

"They've both been accepted to the state college," Mr. Carter continued, "one for this fall and the other on the early-acceptance program for the following year, provided she keeps her grades up."

Mr. Carter stopped as though he wasn't quite sure of what to say next, and Otis said, "You must be very proud of them."

"Oh yes, we are, but our problem is trying to make a way for them to go. Our church has given them each a small scholarship, and I've managed to get some donations from several local businessmen. But we're still short some, enough to keep them out."

Otis began to listen more carefully.

"My grandson was playing one of your records—he really likes you—and he mentioned that you were a Macon boy, too. Well, it occurred to me that maybe you'd be in a position to help us out a bit, if you were willing."

Mr. Carter handed Otis the pile of papers. "Now, I know you must get a lot of requests for money, and you're probably wondering just how legitimate this all is. So I brought along copies of their acceptance letters from the college and their high school grades and the recommendations from their principal and the pastor."

Otis could tell that the youngsters had certainly done well. He felt very strongly about people getting as much education as they possibly could—one of the things he'd always regretted was that he'd dropped out of high school. Sure, he'd been lucky enough to make a real good living anyway, but there were a lot of things he just didn't know, and having money wouldn't bring him the knowledge he knew he needed.

That was why Otis had been one of the most enthusiastic members of the group when Vice-President Humphrey had asked the Stax-Volt stars to make a *Stay in School* album: it gave him a chance to say how he felt about education to a lot of young people.

So Otis decided to do what he could for the Carter grandchildren. He arranged for Mr. Carter to talk with the lawyer who managed Otis' finances so that they could set up a fund to provide money, as needed, for the youngsters' education.

There was only one limitation on the agreement—Mr. Carter had to agree to keep everything completely confidential.

"I'm doing this to help these kids' education, not to build up my own reputation," Otis told Mr. Carter. "After all," he continued, smiling, "I hope I can do that with my singing."

But Otis' concern for others was always a part of his reputation, no matter how little he himself made of it.

Chapter 9

NEW HORIZONS

Early in 1967 Phil had some exciting news. For several months a couple of European concert promoters had been trying to negotiate a European tour for Otis. It seemed that his records were doing even better in Europe than they were in this country, and "Otis fever" was building there.

It had taken Phil quite a while to convince the promotors that Otis Redding working with a strange back-up group was one thing while Otis Redding working with the MG's and the Mar-Keys was something else again. Finally, with the big brass at Stax-Volt, they put together a Stax-Volt package starring Otis and including the MG's and Mar-Keys, and sold the idea to the Europeans. After all, if they were going to all that trouble and expense, why not do it right and get the full impact of that special Memphis sound and feeling?

Otis and Phil were looking forward to the tour, but

in spite of the fact that Otis' records were going very well in Europe, they were worried about how the audiences would respond to "live" performances. Sure, Otis' recordings were gutsy and honest and strong, but his in-person appearances depended almost entirely on the interaction between Otis and his audience. Without those rocking vibrations—a certain tension-and-release that Otis got going with his listeners—his performance might fall flat.

"I've heard that those European concert audiences can be sorta stiff," Otis said to Phil one afternoon when they were discussing the tour.

"Not as stiff as they used to be," Phil replied. "They've been known to get kind of worked up over the Beatles and the Rolling Stones."

Otis thought about that. "Maybe you're right, but what we do is the real thing, and what those guys do—no matter how good it is—is only sort of a cleaner version of our thing. Maybe we'll be too raw for those folks."

"Well, Otis, you'll just have to be prepared to sock it to them and not let things fall apart if they don't jam with you like they do here," Phil said quietly. "But if anyone can get them to let loose, it'll be you."

Otis wasn't too reassured by that, because he really counted on audience reaction to generate the emotion that made his shows so exciting and inspired him to put even more of himself into his act. But, he told himself, if they can't feel what's happening when I get out there with the MG's and the Mar-Keys they'd have to be dead, and I can't believe anybody could be *that* dead.

They were scheduled to do concerts in England, France, Germany, and the Scandinavian countries, and everyone involved in the tour, not just Phil and Otis, was a little worried about the response. But by the time Otis bounded out on the stage of Filsbury Hall in London, their first show, he knew everything was going to be all right. The rest of the acts in the package had set the scene, and the audience was relaxed and ready to get into the Otis Redding groove.

Otis broke into the Beatles' "Day Tripper." Five seconds later the audience picked up the beat and began clapping rhythmically. By the time the band cut back into the second round of the song, the place was rocking as wildly as any Otis had played in Georgia.

"What was that we were saying about European audiences?" Otis demanded of Phil when he ran offstage for a minute to mop his brow after his second number.

"Man, I told you if anybody could move 'em, you could," Phil replied, shaking his head.

"Yeah—they understand the feeling. That's where it's

at. I could tell halfway through the first number. What this audience is digging is the *spirit* of the thing."

When Otis returned to the stage, the theater filled with whistles, shouts, and clapping, and when he launched into "I've Been Loving You Too Long" the audience seemed to float right into the bluesy mood.

Audiences *were* tuned in to Otis Redding's music. They liked what they felt, and it didn't make any difference if they were American, English, or French, whether they could understand the lyrics or not. They dug the spirit of the thing, as Otis had said.

He continued to win European audiences wherever he appeared. In Oslo, Norway, the fans not only gave him a standing ovation, but they were standing on their seats when they did it. By the time the tour was over, European music critics were agreeing that as far as they were concerned, Otis Redding was the most original, most entertaining rhythm and blues singer performing.

Before Otis returned to the States, various European radio and television stations were making arrangements to do special programs on him. Later, the British Broadcasting Corporation sent a crew to America and filmed an hour-long documentary on Otis, his life, his work, and his family. A French radio station broadcast a series of four weekly programs on Otis which included taped interviews with him that had been translated into French.

Otis Redding had taken Europe by storm, but back in his home country it was the same old story. Although his performances had been front-page news in France, there was hardly a mention of his overseas success in the American R&B magazines. Although he had been featured on major TV and radio specials in England, he very seldom appeared on American television, and then only on teen dance shows. It seemed that his own country wasn't taking his musical talent and performing genius seriously.

Until that happened, the Otis Redding Plan was incomplete.

The year 1967 was turning into a very interesting one all the way around. There was a lot of activity in Otis' business world. For one thing, Otis and Phil were partners in Otis Redding Enterprises. Walco Music Company had been handling both music publishing and talent promotion, but the talent end of the operation became so active that they'd started Otis Redding Enterprises so they'd have a business outlet that did nothing but manage and promote the promising new young artists they discovered. It was keeping them busy.

For another thing, for quite a while Otis had wanted to set up a recording studio in Macon so that they wouldn't have to troop up to Stax-Volt in Memphis every time they wanted to cut a demo on one of their discoveries. He had now done so, and the recording end of the business was called Big O Enterprises. Their first production was a catchy tune recorded by Billy Young called "The Sloppy," and Otis and Phil were putting a lot into a regional promotional effort.

For yet another thing, shortly after Otis returned from the European tour there was another interesting but maybe worrisome offer to perform in a new setting.

Otis and Phil were discussing the offer when Zelma walked into the living room of the Redding home with a couple of cool drinks and handed one to Otis and the other to Phil, who was stretched out on the couch.

"Whatever you're thinking about, it sure must be heavy," she commented as she turned to leave the room. "Boy, do you two look puzzled."

As usual, Zelma was right. They *were* puzzled.

"Who did you say called?" Otis asked Phil.

"His name is John Phillips, one of the producers of this pop festival they're gonna do out at Monterey," Phil answered. "He says he really digs your music and so does his partner, Lou Adler, and that they and several other members of the planning committee definitely want you to appear at the festival."

Otis knew about the annual jazz and folk festivals that had been started a few years earlier in Monterey, California, but this was something new.

"Well, I don't know—I'm not sure how I'd go over with a pop audience. They're all into plain rock and roll and that's not my bag," Otis commented.

"I'm hip," Phil said. "And besides, they want you to work for nothing. This first year, Phillips said, they're asking the artists to perform for free to get the thing off the ground. He says they're gonna sink all their bread into heavy promotion and publicity."

"It *better* be heavy. California's quite a way—just getting there will be an investment." Otis looked doubtful. "I don't know . . ." he said again, letting the sentence trail off.

"Look, let's call Jerry Wexler and see what he thinks about all this," Phil suggested. "Then we can get our heads together better."

Otis agreed, and while Phil was making the call to Wexler, a vice-president of Atlantic Records (which distributed the Stax-Volt sides) and a close friend of both Phil and Otis, he muddled over the idea.

Phil talked for quite a while, then hung up.

"What'd Jerry say?" Otis asked.

"He thinks it would probably be a good thing for you to go. All the acts will be professionally recorded, he says, and he's heard they're going to film the whole thing. There'll probably be a mob of people there. He thinks it might be worth it to you to get that kind of exposure, but that we should consider the no-pay angle very carefully before we make up our minds."

"You bet," Otis said firmly.

A few days later they talked to Jerry Wexler again. He was more sure of himself now. The festival seemed legitimate, he said, and the folk and jazz festivals held at Monterey always received quite a bit of attention in the press, both in the music trade and in national magazines, and they were generally well run. Also, none of the performers was going to be paid, and there were some pretty big names scheduled to appear, so it wouldn't be a put-down to Otis' status.

Otis, Phil, and Speedo got together to make the final decision.

"Just remember," Speedo said, "it's not going to be a soul audience—mostly white kids who might not dig what you're into."

"That's the same kind of worry we had about Europe," Otis replied. "Didn't seem to stop them from grooving with us once they heard us."

"Sure," Phil countered, "but at least the Europeans

had been buying your records and liking them before you got there. These kids at Monterey probably won't even have heard of you."

Otis was thinking. "But according to Wexler the festival will get good press coverage. Isn't that what I need most at this point?"

"Well, O, that's true, but what if the audience was dead and nothing happened? You sure you'd want a lot of press coverage on *that* kind of reaction?" Speedo asked.

Otis grinned. His mind was made up. "Look, I think we can take that chance, don't you, really? They haven't met us yet, and we haven't met them—and it seems to me like it's about time for us to get together."

Phil and Speedo still weren't completely in favor of Otis going to Monterey, but Otis reminded them that Lou Rawls and Jimi Hendrix were supposed to appear, so at least he wouldn't be the *only* soul act out there, even if he and Hendrix and Rawls were into different bags. Also, they'd try to get Booker T and the MG's as the back-up group, and if that worked out—well, there really couldn't be any serious objection.

Finally, Otis said, "Remember a long time ago I told you, Phil, that I'd sing any time, anywhere? Well, that still holds. I see that audience out there in Monterey as a real challenge, man, even more than Europe. And

I'm going to sock it to them harder than I socked it to those folks overseas.

"And you know something else?" Otis asked with a little smile as he got up and headed for the door. "I know it's gonna turn out just fine."

Booker T and the MG's agreed to make it, and that settled it for everybody—Phil and Speedo decided they were as much in favor of Otis' Monterey appearance as Otis himself was.

The Monterey festivals—jazz, folk, and pop—not only present the best in their kinds of music, but present it in a wildly beautiful outdoor setting on the Monterey Peninsula on the California coast. When Otis and Phil first saw it on Saturday morning, June 17, they felt even better about being there, because it seemed like such a good atmosphere to relax and listen in, and perform in. The festival was in its second day, and everything seemed to be going well.

Temporary facilities had been set up for the performers at the rear of the stage, and Otis, Phil, Booker Jones, and the rest of the MG's gathered there to go over their program. Otis was scheduled to be the final act on the Saturday evening show.

Last billing was usually an honored spot, saved for the headliner. In this case, however, performing last seemed to put Otis at a disadvantage. It was going to be a long night of music, and maybe the audience wouldn't wait till the end of the show just to hear somebody named Otis Redding. Phil complained to the management, but it was too late to do anything about it—they'd just have to hope for the best.

Otis and Phil watched that evening as the various groups went through their acts. Lou Rawls was enthusiastically received and came back for several more numbers.

Otis began to worry. After all, the audience was bound to be tired of listening to so much music. Furthermore, the weather had turned chilly. Monterey was right on the ocean, and a cold fog was blowing in off the water.

How was he going to handle a crowd that had been sitting out in the cold listening to music for two days? Otis wondered. Then it hit him: he'd just go out there and make them feel good. He'd do everything he could to warm them up, cheer them up, "soul" them up until they forgot about the cold, the time, and everything else.

It was after midnight when Booker T and his unit finally went out on stage. They did a couple of numbers, just enough to set the mood. Then the Big O stomped out, his suit shining in the lights, looking ten feet tall.

Otis said a few words to the crowd: "They tell me

this is the love generation. Let's see what you can do with all that love." And then he went into Sam Cooke's "Shake":

> Shake! Ah-ah-ah-oh-oh-oh-oh-oh!
> Shake! Ah-ah-ah-oh-oh-oh-oh-oh!
> Shake! Ah-ah-ah-oh-oh-oh-oh-oh!

Four bars later, the whole crowd was on its feet, shaking, clapping, shouting. Otis kept jamming "shake" into the mike and the audience forgot all about the cold, the time, the damp, and everything else.

Otis and Booker T cooked through "Respect," and then did Otis' soulful ballad "I've Been Loving You Too Long." After that they socked out "Satisfaction" like nobody had ever heard it done before. Otis felt so good he could have sung all night, but the management was concerned that the show was running so late. So, after "Satisfaction" came to its roaring end, the evening was officially over.

But the crowd was really "souled up" and they just weren't going for that. After five minutes of steady clapping, stomping, and calling, Otis stormed back out for an encore, "Try a Little Tenderness":

> You gotta, gotta, gotta
> Na, na, na, na, na,
> You gotta try a little tenderness.

Oh yes, Lord, have mercy now.
Come on and do it, take my advice,
You gotta hold her, squeeze her, never leave her,
Na, na, na, na, na, na, na . . .

The Redding sound poured out over the festival grounds. Otis wasn't doing anything different in Monterey than he'd been doing all along in Macon or Roanoke or Jackson—or London or Paris or Oslo. The difference was that up until now, this audience had never heard Otis Redding do his thing. The whole area took on the spirit of a revival meeting.

Here's how writer Pete Johnson described Otis' performance that night:

> Within moments after Otis Redding hit the stage, the crowd was on its feet and—for the first and only time in a weekend of five massive concerts—was impulsively moving toward the stage to dance in the warmth of his fire. He rocked and rolled past the curfew with a dazzling performance which no one could think of stopping. That night he gave the Monterey International Pop Festival its high point and he was embraced by the rock crowd as a new-found hero.

The next day Otis began receiving messages and telegrams of praise. *Esquire, Time,* and other national publications didn't write about the Monterey festival that year—they wrote about Otis Redding at the Monterey festival; as *Downbeat* magazine said, "To Otis Redding went the most tumultuous audience reception of the festival." The American music world was now truly discovering the Redding talent.

Booking offers poured in from famous nightclubs and concert halls. And other American performers began to pay attention, too. When Otis later played at Basin Street West in San Francisco, for example, Bob Dylan came to see him perform four nights in a row, and Janis Joplin later said she liked Otis' singing better than anybody else's.

As Otis had predicted, performing at Monterey had turned out "just fine."

Chapter 10

GOAL IN SIGHT

After the wildly successful Monterey Pop Festival, Otis had to come back down to earth, and he did it by means of more hard work all during the summer of 1967—more tours, recording, songwriting, business arrangements. He was also busy with plans to open a camp for under-privileged boys, to be located on his ranch.

He was working on those plans with his secretary in his office one morning when the phone rang. His secretary answered, listened, and then said, "Yes, operator, Mr. Redding is right here." To Otis she whispered, "It's from London—one of the editors of *Melody Maker* wants to talk to you."

Otis looked interested but a little perplexed. He knew it was about time for *Melody Maker*, the leading British pop-music magazine, to announce the outcome of the poll they conducted each year to select what they called the "Top Ten Male Singers in the World," but a cable would have done the job if they were informing him of the results. Elvis Presley had won the poll for the past ten years. True, Otis had come in seventh in 1966, but Elvis seemed to have permanent possession of first place. So why the call?

"They're *still* talking about your tour over here," the British voice said after they had exchanged greetings, "but that's not what I'm calling about. Or maybe, in a way, it is."

"Yes?" Otis said politely.

"In any case, I'm delighted to inform you that you have won first place in our annual poll—you've been named the number-one male vocalist for 1967."

Otis wanted to be cool, but all he could manage was, "You must be kidding!"

"Oh, not at all," the *Melody Maker* editor laughed, and went on to explain that Otis would be receiving formal notification of the honor within the next forty-eight hours. Moreover, the magazine would be sending a writer over to interview Otis. The Englishman was explaining other details about the award, but Otis hardly heard a word.

After he had hung up, Otis sat back in his chair, his mind blank except for the single sentence going around in his head: "They've voted me number one in the world. They've voted me number one in the world."

Then suddenly he came to and dashed down the hall to Phil's office. Phil nearly leaped over the desk when he heard the news. Pretty soon everyone in Walco was crowding into Phil's office, and within half an hour Zelma and the children arrived.

Phil sent out for refreshments and they had an impromptu party on the spot. Sprawled out in one of the office armchairs, Otis still had a sort of blank look of disbelief on his face.

"Well, man," Phil said, "it looks like you've made it now, right on top where you want to be."

"Yeah, man, almost," Otis replied. "But not quite."

Being named number one in the *Melody Maker* poll was beautiful, but it still didn't represent full recognition of Otis Redding by his own countrymen. It had to happen—and big—all over the United States for his dream to come true.

So that fall the entire team continued to push to make Otis better known throughout the country. Ralph Gleason, the noted San Francisco music critic, invited Otis to San Francisco to do a series of shows in the area and work at a number of first-rate West Coast nightclubs.

Otis hadn't had an opportunity to get to San Francisco when he'd been at Monterey, so this was his first chance to see the sights of the city. He and Phil wanted to be able to relax as well as work while they were there, so they rented a houseboat on San Francisco Bay. Of course, they worked *while* they relaxed, and Otis used the time to write some new songs, usually while he was lying comfortably on the deck of the boat. It was while he was there that he first observed the young people who then were known as "flower children," the hippies who hung out around the waterfront. For a driving, hard-working man like Otis, their style of life was disturbing. "Man, look at them," he said to Phil. "They're throwing their lives away, just hanging around wasting time."

Gradually during his stay in San Francisco, a tune started buzzing in his head, something different from anything he'd worked on before. It was sort of a ballad, but it wasn't anything like his pounding blues ballads such as "These Arms of Mine" or "I've Been Loving You Too Long."

Otis thought about it after the song occurred to him —if he was going to reach a wider audience, like those kids who were hanging around San Francisco, like the audience at the Monterey festival—*really* reach them, that is—he was going to have to integrate his soul sound and style with something that spoke to their experience more directly. Otis sensed that the time would soon

come when soul and folk and hard rock and all the different kinds of pop music wouldn't be such rigid catego-
ries, when performers would be able to do different
kinds of material and reach more people without losing
their basic audience. He wanted to try it—and even if
he hadn't wanted to, this new song wouldn't let him go.
But he *did* want to; he welcomed the song. However,
his new direction didn't light many fires with his business colleagues.

Otis was singing the opening lines of the song to himself in his office when Speedo came in one afternoon in
November. He still didn't have the number together,
but it was getting there:

> Left my home in Georgia
> Headed for the Frisco Bay,
> Now I've got nothing to live for,
> Seems like nothing's going to come my way . . .

Speedo watched as Otis stopped, corrected a few no-
tations, and began the tune again. He'd never heard Otis
doing anything like that before.

"Hey, man, what are you doing—going folk on us?"
he asked good-naturedly.

Otis waved one hand, indicating that he didn't want
to be disturbed, so Speedo listened quietly as Otis

worked on the song. Finally, Otis looked up from the piano.

"Where'd you get that from?" Speedo asked.

"Where does it look like I'm getting it from? From my head, from inside me," Otis retorted. "It may not sound like 'me,'" he explained, "but it's a new direction I want to try. Well, not an entirely new direction—more like a new way that's coming out of the old."

Speedo shook his head doubtfully. "I don't know—when people think of Otis Redding, they think of 'Respect' and 'Satisfaction.' That's the kind of numbers your fans dig, not something with a whole lot of words."

"How do you know?" Otis asked. "They haven't ever heard me *do* anything like this—so how do we know how they'll react?"

"Do Phil and Alan or any of the others know about this?"

"Not yet," Otis answered. "There's nothing to tell till I get it worked out."

And with that, he turned back to the piano.

Later, Otis decided to stop by Alan's house on his way home. "Might as well return this," he said to himself, picking up a new Beatles album, *Sergeant Pepper*.

Otis was notorious for borrowing records and never returning them; some of his friends swore that he'd never bought an album in his life. Therefore Alan was glad to see Otis, but even gladder to see his album.

"This new stuff the Beatles are doing is all right—really interesting," Otis said as he handed the record to Alan.

"Well, it's sort of gimmicky, don't you think—all those electronic effects?"

"No, I don't," Otis replied. "Lennon and McCartney are really fine writers—they'll be around for a long time. And I think the electronic effects bring out the true nature of their music. I'm like you—when I first heard about the album I thought, man, that sounds like a big, unnecessary deal. But once I started listening, I could hear and feel how it works. It got to me."

"Lord, I hope you're not gonna turn into the Memphis version of the Beatles!" Alan exclaimed.

"No—not quite. But I *have* been working on something sort of different from my usual thing. You want to hear it?"

Of course Alan did, so Otis unpacked his guitar and ran through the new, quiet song for him.

"It's sort of a nice tune, O," Alan said when Otis finished and looked at him, waiting for Alan's reaction. "But it's not *you*, it's not what people want to hear from you. Unless you're going to give it the old Redding soul treatment," he added hopefully.

"First of all," Otis replied, a little tired, "it's as much me as anything else. I felt it and I'm writing it and I still feel it. If that isn't me, what is?"

Alan shrugged.

"Second of all," Otis went on, "I'm going to do it the way I feel it and the way the *song* feels. There's lots of ways to express soul, you know. As a matter of fact, I always feel like whistling at the end of it, and that's what I think I'll do when I record it."

"Oh, man, wait till Phil hears about this," Alan sighed. "Wait till *Galkin* hears about it. Wow."

As Alan expected, neither Phil nor Joe Galkin was very enthusiastic about the number, but there wasn't much time to argue with Otis about it because his schedule was so tight he was really on the run the next week, the first week in December. He was so busy, in fact, that he couldn't even find time to finish working on the song himself.

From Monday to Wednesday, he hoped to catch up on work at Walco, which was piled to the ceiling. On Thursday he was scheduled to fly to Memphis to finish recording an album they were thinking of calling the *History of Otis Redding* because he was redoing some of his hits from throughout his career so far. He was going to stay in Memphis for a show on Friday night, then fly to Cleveland for a performance on Saturday.

On Sunday morning they'd all fly to Madison, Wisconsin, for a show there that evening.

On Monday, the schedule started to fall apart.

"Mr. Redding, there's a letter from the White House in the mail this morning," his secretary announced excitedly as she handed Otis an envelope from the stack on her desk.

Otis read the letter standing right there. It was from Vice-President Humphrey, inviting the Redding show to entertain the troops in Vietnam early in 1968. Instead of going into his own office, Otis went to tell Phil the news, and they ended up spending the whole day making preliminary plans for the tour.

It was complicated, because it meant reworking the plans they'd already made. Otis was booked to play a Christmas show in San Francisco, and immediately after that he was scheduled to film an hour-long documentary on his career and singing style for the National Educational Television network. In addition, there were a whole series of concerts that had to be shifted around and worked in someplace else.

By Wednesday night, Otis was a tired man. He knew that the recording session wasn't going to be as easy as usual because he intended to record the new tune, which he was now calling "Dock of the Bay," and he was sure he'd have to hassle with some of the Stax-

Volt people who'd be upset about his "image" if he did the song. On top of that, he hadn't had time to work out everything about the song he wanted to, and so he wasn't really ready to record it—but he was determined to do it anyway. And on top of *that*, they were working on material for more than one album, and it was bound to be a very long session.

He called Steve Cropper from Macon and asked him to meet him at the studio in Memphis on Thursday morning, as soon as Otis got in.

"Steve, I've got a terriffic new song to do," Otis said when they met at the Stax studios. "I really want to cut it today but I haven't had time to get it together."

"Let's hear it, O," Steve replied.

Steve, being a musician, knew what the song was about the first time he heard it and was as much for recording it as Otis was. They worked in the empty studio for a couple of hours putting the finishing touches on it and getting their ideas for the arrangement clear. They worked well together—as they always did—and by the time the other musicians started drifting in, "Dock of the Bay" was ready.

As it turned out, the recording session didn't go badly. Some of those opposed to "Dock of the Bay" just accepted the fact that Otis was determined to do it, and others really began to dig the song. The rest of the session fell into a good groove. They didn't finish everything, but felt they could easily wrap it all up the following week, after the group returned from Madison.

Otis was happy to become Otis Redding, performer, again when he strutted out onto the stage in Memphis on Friday night, and again in Cleveland on Saturday. Both the Memphis and Cleveland audiences were with him all the way, and by the end of the show in Cleveland Otis was feeling his very best. All the tiredness of the week was gone—there was nothing like an audience to make him feel better.

Early Sunday morning Otis was wakened by the phone in his hotel room.

"Otis? This is Dick Frazier. Have you taken a look outside yet? The weather's terrible—the worst kind for flying. Raining, foggy. I checked with the weather bureau, and they say it's like this all the way west to Madison."

Otis rubbed his eyes. "What you're saying is that we can't fly to Madison?"

"That's what I'm saying," Dick replied with a sigh.

"Do they think it'll last all day?"

"I'm afraid so—until tomorrow."

Otis thought for a minute. "We're all meeting downstairs for breakfast in an hour. Let's discuss it then."

It was a glum group that assembled for breakfast that morning: Ben Cauley, Phalon Jones, Ronnie Caldwell, Jimmy King, and Carl Cunningham of the Mar-Keys, their valet Matthew Kelley, pilot Dick Frazier, and Otis.

This was the first time they'd been grounded since they started using the plane. It especially bugged Otis because it was just such delays that he'd hoped to avoid by having his own plane. Now here they were, stranded in Cleveland on a rainy Sunday.

"This is sure a letdown after that good gig last night," Carl complained.

"Yeah, man, but what are we gonna do?" Ronnie said.

Otis turned to Dick. "Don't we have radar equipment to get through stuff like this?"

"Sure we do. But it's not a good idea to put too much faith in your instruments, especially in weather this bad."

Otis stared down at his plate, arms folded across his chest. So far he'd kept his promise to himself: he'd never missed a performance. He just couldn't accept the thought of missing a gig after all these years.

"Explain to me a little about how the radar instruments work," Otis said to Dick, who gave him a brief rundown of the radar system in the Beechcraft.

"I'm supposed to have one of the best small planes you can buy," Otis announced. "Therefore, it seems to me it should be able to get us to Madison."

"We can try, of course," Dick responded, "but as your pilot, I'm advising you to forget it. What's so important about making this date, anyway?"

"You wouldn't understand."

Otis got up. "C'mon, we'll make it okay. Let's get ready to go. The folks in Madison are waiting."

Otis sat in the co-pilot's as usual. The Mar-Keys laughed and joked a little nervously as the plane shuddered in the choppy weather. Dick Frazier leaned forward, staring at the instrument control panel. Otis tried talking to him throughout the flight, but Dick remained tensely silent.

Suddenly, when they were almost there, the plane lurched, and then streaked groundward. With a roaring crash, it plunged into icy Lake Pomona outside of Madison. Of all the passengers, only Ben Cauley survived.

On December 10, 1967, the career of Otis Redding, Jr., age twenty-six, was over, his dream ended.

Chapter 11

EULOGY

As news of the tragedy reached the public, expressions of grief began to pour into Macon from all over the world. Rock and R&B publications quickly put together memorial issues to honor Otis Redding. Radio stations all over the world broadcast tributes to the dead singer, some of them playing all of Otis' records, from the beginning of his career to its premature end.

In Macon, Georgia, the town Otis had loved so much, preparations were begun for a hero's funeral. Hundreds of Otis' friends, from both the small world of Macon and the large world of show business, wanted to attend the services, and so the Macon City Auditorium was reserved as the place where last respects would be paid to Otis.

On December 18, 1967, the auditorium was filled with both white and black mourners. Although the hall could seat only thirty-six hundred people, more than four thousand were crammed into every available space, and there were nearly fifteen hundred more outside who could not get in.

The service lasted fifty minutes. Reverend C. J. Andrews of the Vineville Baptist Church gave a stirring eulogy. Jerry Wexler broke down as he tried to explain what Otis' friendship had meant to him. Ronnie Thompson, the mayor of Macon, called the entertainer "Macon's ambassador of goodwill." State Senator Leroy Johnson also spoke at the service, revealing for the first time the contributions Otis Redding had made to scholarships for needy students and black voter-registration drives.

The music at the service was the kind Otis had often sung himself in his father's church: Joe Simon gave his rendition of "Jesus Nearer to the Cross," and Johnny Taylor sang "I'll Be Standing By," with Booker T. Jones playing the organ.

Then the pallbearers—among them Joe Tex, Joe Simon, Johnny Taylor, Earl "Speedo" Sims, and Otis' brother, Roger—carried the casket out into the Georgia sun. The procession which followed slowly after them included some of the biggest names in the popular-music world: James Brown, Little Richard, Fats Domino, Wilson Pickett, Sam and Dave, Percy Sledge, Aretha Franklin, Stevie Wonder, Arthur Conley, Jamo Thomas,

Don Covay, Johnny Williams, Solomon Burke, Mabel John—and many, many others.

Otis Redding inspired some moving tributes from those who worked with him and from others who were gripped by his artistry as a performer.

Marty Balin, with the Jefferson Airplane, said it most simply: "Otis Redding was the sky and the clouds and the sunshine. He really was."

Critic Ralph Gleason: "Otis Redding was a remarkable, multi-talented artist . . . who not only sang the blues but carried over into everything he did some aspects of the blues sound and feeling. . . . His emotional message, his charisma, his total effect, was instantaneous. . . . In person, everything Redding did was an all-out, powerhouse, emotional explosion. His effect on American popular music was fundamental. . . . He was a tremendous force."

Robert Shelton, pop-music critic of the New York *Times:* "The death of Otis Redding . . . was a major loss to the pop-music world. Coming at a time when his career as singer, composer, manager, and personality were all towering, his death seemed particularly premature. . . . Redding as a recording artist was a powerful figure, but his true magic came alive on the stage, where a torrent of motion, gesture, and total involvement would be unleashed as he built his patterns in sound. . . . One always believed that he was centrally involved in the emotions of his songs."

Recording executive Jerry Wexler: "Otis Redding was a natural prince. When you were with him he communicated love and a tremendous faith in human possibility, a promise that great and happy events were coming. In some magic way his recordings have the same inspirational quality. . . . 'Dock of the Bay' is Otis' epitaph, and it proves that a singer can do his own thing and still be commercially successful. Otis is tremendously responsible for the fact that so much of the young white audience now digs soul the way the black audience does."

Rock critic Jon Landau, who has written some of the most perceptive articles on Otis and was deeply involved in his music: "Words cannot begin to pay adequate tribute to what Otis Redding accomplished in the few short years he was an entertainer. The real tribute rests in the permanent impression his creativity has left on American popular music, for future American pop music will be influenced by Redding far more than can be imagined, just as it has been by Sam Cooke.

"Otis Redding's music had the power to make you dig yourself. The people who were really close to Redding's music, the people whose way of life Redding expressed, those people will tell you that is what soul is all about. Otis Redding was the most recent, most influential, and most talented of a long line of soul musicians. He was truly the 'king of them all.'"

But the most moving statement has come from Steve Cropper, guitarist with Booker T and the MG's and a close associate of Otis: "My original feeling for Otis wound up to be my final feeling for Otis. He was a pure man. Anything you say about him has to be good. He was a good person. He always got along well with the people around him . . . and it showed up in his records and in his work. When Otis came in to work, he turned everybody on. He put so much into it. . . .

"He always gave the musicians credit for everything that he did. If he had a hit record, he'd tell us, 'Man, I couldn't make it if it weren't for you.' . . . He always wanted to give somebody else credit for helping him. You can't help but like people like that. . . .

"I learned a lot from just being with him. I can't think of a particular thing he taught me, it was just the experience of working with him. The main thing I got from Otis was the fired interest in working on something. He always had the right direction. . . .

"The accident hit everybody. . . . It was a loss to the whole world. Now nobody will know what he had in store for them. He was just starting to come into something, to get out of hard rhythm and blues. He went beyond that. He was hitting everybody all over the world."

The *History of Otis Redding* album was released very soon after Otis' death. The public was stunned by the irony of the title, as well as by the strong music in the album, which spanned Otis' recording career in vital new renditions of his biggest hits.

But even more, listeners were stirred by the beauty and uniqueness of a new single, also released shortly after Otis died: "Dock of the Bay." This was a different Otis Redding, one they hadn't known before. And the public liked what it heard. Just three months after its release, the record had sold 1,400,000 copies. The treasured gold record was presented to Zelma Redding in honor of Otis.

Zelma accepted many other tributes in Otis' name. The National Academy of Recording Arts and Sciences nominated Otis' version of "Try a Little Tenderness" as the Best Male Solo Rhythm and Blues Recording of 1967. Both the Georgia House and Senate passed resolutions declaring Otis Redding to have been a great citizen of the state, and expressing formal regret at his passing.

Otis Redding was buried on his ranch, the Big O.

His memory is kept alive by the many recordings he left behind, but especially his last one:

> Roamed two thousand miles from Georgia,
> Never to go back home again. . . .
> Oh, sitting on the dock of the bay,
> Watching the tide roll away,
> Sitting on the dock of the bay,
> Wasting time.

OTIS REDDING'S ALBUMS

Following is a list of albums by Otis Redding which are still available.

Stax-Volt was taken over by Atlantic Records a few years ago, and so the albums that were originally released on the Volt label are now on Atco.

PAIN IN MY HEART (*Atco 33–161*)

Pain in My Heart / The Dog / Stand By Me / Hey, Hey, Baby / You Send Me / I Need Your Lovin' / Louie, Louie / Security / These Arms of Mine / Something Is Worrying Me / That's What My Heart Needs / Lucille

THE GREAT OTIS REDDING SINGS SOUL BALLADS (*Atco 33–248*)

That's How Strong My Love Is / Chained and Bound / Mr. Pitiful / Woman, Lover, a Friend / Your One

and Only Man / Nothing Can Change This Love /
For Your Precious Love / It's Too Late / I Want to
Thank You / Come to Me / Home in Your Heart
/ Keep Your Arms Around Me

DICTIONARY OF SOUL (*Atco 33–249*)

Day Tripper / Tennessee Waltz / My Lover's Prayer
/ Fa Fa Fa Fa Fa (Sad Song) / I'm Sick, Y'All /
Sweet Lorraine / Try a Little Tenderness / She Put
the Hurt on Me / Ton of Joy / You're Still My Baby
/ Hawg for You / Love, Have Mercy

THE IMMORTAL OTIS REDDING (*Atco 33–252*)

I've Got Dreams to Remember / You Made a Man
Out of Me / Nobody's Fault But Mine / Hard to
Handle / Think About It / The Happy Song (Dum
Dum De De De Dum Dum) / A Waste of Time /
Champagne and Wine / A Fool for You / Amen /
A Thousand Miles Away

HISTORY OF OTIS REDDING (*Atco 33–261*)

I've Been Loving You Too Long / Try a Little Tenderness / Shake / These Arms of Mine / Pain in
My Heart / My Lover's Prayer / Fa Fa Fa Fa Fa

(Sad Song) / Respect / Satisfaction / Mr. Pitiful
/ Security / I Can't Turn You Loose

IN PERSON AT THE WHISKEY-A-GO-GO
(*Atco 33–265*)

Just One More Day / I Can't Turn You Loose / Pain
in My Heart / Mr. Pitiful / These Arms of Mine /
Any Ol' Way / I'm Depending on You / Satisfaction
/ Poppa's Got a Brand-New Bag / Respect

OTIS BLUE (*Atco 33–248*)

Ol' Man Trouble / Respect / Change Gonna Come
/ My Girl / Down in the Valley / I've Been Loving
You Too Long / Shake / Satisfaction / You Don't
Miss the Water / Wonderful World / Rock Me,
Baby

THE SOUL ALBUM (*Atco 33–285*)

Just One More Day / It's Growing / Cigarettes and
Coffee / Chain Gang / Nobody Knows You When
You're Down and Out / Good to Me / Scratch My
Back / Treat Her Right / Everybody Makes a Mis-
take / Any Ol' Way / 634–5789

"LIVE" IN EUROPE (*Atco* 33–286)

Respect / I Can't Turn You Loose / I've Been Loving You Too Long / My Girl / Shake / These Arms of Mine / Satisfaction / Fa Fa Fa Fa Fa (Sad Song) / Day Tripper / Try a Little Tenderness

DOCK OF THE BAY (*Atco* 33–288)

Dock of the Bay / Tramp / I Love You More Than Words Can Say / Let Me Come On Home / Open the Door / Don't Mess with Cupid / Glory of Love / I'm Coming Home / Huckle-Buck / Nobody Knows You When You're Down and Out / Ol' Man Trouble

LOVE MAN (*Atco* 33–289)

Love Man / Higher and Higher / I'm a Changed Man / That's a Good Idea / I'll Let Nothing Separate Us / Direct Me / Groovin' Time / Lovers' Question / The Feeling Is Mine / Got to Get Myself Together / Free Me / Look at That Girl

TELL THE TRUTH (*Atco* 33–333)

Tell the Truth / Demonstration / Out of Sight / Give Away None of My Life / Wholesale Love / I Got the Will / Johnny's Heartbreak / Snatch a Little Piece / Slippin' and Slidin' / The Match Game / A Little Time / Swingin' on a String

KING AND QUEEN—With Carla Thomas (*Stax 7716*)

Knock on Wood / Tramp / Let Me Be Good to You / Tell It Like It Is / When Something Is Wrong with My Baby / Lovey Dovey / New Year's Resolution / It Takes Two / Are You Lonely for Me, Baby? / Bring It on Home to Me / Ooh Carla, Ooh Otis

HERE COMES SOME SOUL (*Alshire 5082*)

Gettin' Hip / Your Mini Skirt / Gamma Lama / Let Me Make It Up to You / PLUS SIX NUMBERS BY JOE CURTIS

OTIS REDDING AT THE MONTEREY POP FESTIVAL (*Reprise 2029*)

Shake / Respect / I've Been Loving You Too Long / Satisfaction / Try a Little Tenderness / PLUS FOUR NUMBERS BY JIMI HENDRIX